GET
YES
WITH YOUR BANKER

A PRACTICAL GUIDE FOR SMALL BUSINESS OWNERS

RON STURGEON & GREG MORSE

93 Secrets

Plus 31 traps to avoid and 76 tips to get your business funded

Published by
Mike French Publishing
1619 Front Street
Lynden, WA 98264
Voice: 360.354.8326 Fax: 360.354.3013
mike@mikefrench.com

First edition: May 2011

Sturgeon, Ron and Morse, Greg.
Getting to yes with your banker : a practical guide for small business owners, 93 secrets to getting your small business funded plus 76 tips and 51 traps to avoid / by Ron Sturgeon and Greg Morse. -- 1st ed.
p. cm.
Includes bibliographical references and index.
ISBN 978-0-9717031-6-2 (alk. paper)
1. Small business--United States--Finance. 2. Commercial loans--United States. 3. Business planning. I. Title.
HG4027.7.S875 2011
658.15'224--dc22

2010032447

Dedications

Ron Sturgeon

I would like to dedicate this book to all the people smarter than me who I have surrounded myself with and who do things I shouldn't, wouldn't or couldn't do. This book would not have been possible without Brian and Clint, both of whom taught me so much about lending. A special thank you to all the other bankers who taught me what they wanted to see, know, understand and hear about a business before making a decision to loan. Thanks to that great teacher—experience—that made me a resilient graduate of the school of hard knocks. And, last but not the least, I dedicate this book to my three grown boys, who challenged, respected and inspired me.

❖ ❖ ❖ ❖ ❖ ❖

Greg Morse

To my parents, who fostered my capacity to be driven and to my children, Logan and Hud, who are my foremost driving force.

Foreword
by
Brian Nerney

When I was in grade school, I thought it would be so much easier at test time if we just had the teacher's answer sheet. Well, school is out and we are now in business. But business is so much better than school, because often, if we just look in the right place, we can get the answer sheet!

"Getting to Yes With Your Banker" not only provides answers on how to get a loan, but by following the recommendations in this book, it will be the loan that will help your business grow and become more successful. The banker that makes a business loan is more than just another banker; they are a partner in your success. Getting a loan can be the best thing for a business, not just because it provides needed growth capital, but because in order to get the loan, the business owner needs to think about the business disciplines that lead to success.

I have known Ron Sturgeon since early in his entrepreneurial career, when he had a small portable building and a few salvage automobiles. Over the years Ron built the business with a combination of infectious energy, a strong sense of urgency and plain hard work. As Ron grew the business, he also successfully bought and integrated other auto recycling yards. Ron built the auto recycling business and sold it to Ford Motor Company as its cornerstone acquisition in a rollup of more than 25 auto recyclers. After the sale of the auto recycling business, Ron bought and started more businesses, two of which were sold to publicly traded companies. None of this would have been possible without lots of money, most of it borrowed from banks.

In borrowing money from the banks, there were challenges. Many told Ron that he could not borrow that much money on a junkyard, much less salvage automobiles. Indeed, the bankers had not made a loan on salvage inventory before. I am guessing that very few, if any, auto recyclers borrowed more money than Ron. When a flood hit, he was the only recycler to get an SBA disaster loan because he could explain the business and prove the value of the inventory. His experience with growing businesses, raising capital with bank loans and three private stock offerings, have helped him understand complex accounting and cash flow with an ability to explain it simply to the bankers. Another challenge was to borrow money to purchase a company losing millions of dollars. Ron also got three SBA loans and helped others get loans, both SBA and conventional, for startups as well as ongoing operations. Ron's experience with getting the "hard to get" loans runs long and deep, and he provides the perspective of how to overcome objections. I have known Ron for many years, and know that his words come from wanting to help others achieve success, as he has done in the past.

If you want to get a loan from a banker, what better person to ask than a highly experienced banker that has made many loans? Greg Morse has almost 25 years of banking experience, and is the CEO and founding member of Worthington National Bank. Greg completed the Southwestern Graduate School of Banking at Southern Methodist University (SMU), holds an MBA from Texas Christian University and a BBA from SMU. Additionally, he has taught MBA and senior level finance classes as an adjunct professor at the University of Texas at Arlington, where he received the Excellence in Teaching Award from UTA. Greg has also been honored as a "40 Under 40" award recipient. Even if you decide not to seek a loan, simply following the business planning and disciplines Greg discusses, as not just a banker, but as a CEO and business owner, will make business better.

In one book you not only get the highly successful entrepreneur's viewpoint, and the experienced, respected banker's answers on how to get to get the loan you are looking for, but you also get a guide on many of the techniques used in successful businesses. "Getting to Yes With Your Banker" is a book I recommend you completely consume for practical ways to make your business better than it is today.

If you were looking for the answer sheet on getting a loan, you found it. The bonus is that if you follow the advice in this book, it will also improve your business. Happy reading.

❖ *Brian Nerney is the Managing Director of Sundial Capital Management, a hedge fund management company. He is also the Chairman of ProFormance Technologies, a company in the automotive engine aftermarket business, and serves as a member of the Board of Directors for three other companies. Brian has founded, acquired, operated and sold businesses in the Aerospace, Automotive, Real Estate, Telecommunications and Information Technologies industries. He holds a masters degree in Aerospace Engineering from Virginia Tech and an MBA from the Wharton School of Business.*

Introduction

Ron Sturgeon

With fewer small business loans being given and fewer community banks to give them, you need to know everything you can about getting to yes with your banker.

This book exists because many of the questions that entrepreneurs and aspiring entrepreneurs ask me are about how to get the money to start or grow a business.

What I know about working with bankers was learned by trial and error. I wish I had had a book like the one that you're holding when I first applied for a small business loan.

Such a book would have given me a much better appreciation for what a banker needs to approve a small business loan and the ways that I can make his or her job easier.

Over the last 30 years, I've borrowed money to start and grow businesses in a variety of industries, and each experience has taught me more about the path to yes.

I'm passionate about business and helping other businesspeople succeed, and glad to share what I have learned.

Apply the principles and advice in these pages and you will be on your way.

Introduction

Greg Morse

Experience is what you get when you didn't get what you wanted. And experience is often the most valuable thing we have to offer. Experience is given and taught from many people. Looking back, my dad was much more influential on me than I could ever have imagined. We often grow up and don't realize who some of our best mentors are until it's too late to thank them. A rancher named Sid Evans taught me how to pull a calf, pull an all-nighter and how to pull off a great business deal. He also taught me that a man can't drown in his own sweat.

I would be remiss if I failed to mention the hundreds of teachers, professors, colleagues, bosses, leaders, employees and friends that have helped me live my dream. At this juncture I also have to extend thanks to the best grammar teacher I ever had, Sammie Slocum. She was a secretary of mine in the late '80s and early '90s. One of the hardest tasks of her career had to be teaching a 25-year-old-plus, hard-headed male how to write a sentence. She even remains a great friend today.

I thank Ron Sturgeon for picking me to help author a book with him. I would also like to thank Jennifer Henderson, who told me I was not crazy to co-author a book with Ron Sturgeon.

I have always believed that my potential is God's gift to me. What I do with my potential is my gift to God.

Credits and Acknowledgments

Writer
Paula Felps

Project Manager
Cindy Baldhoff

Editors
Eric Anderson, Greg Kerr

Advisors
Cheryl Georg, Linda Allen, Bette Filley, Jennifer Henderson

Cover Design
Ron Sturgeon & 99 Designs.com

Illustrations
Gahan Wilson from *Green Weenies* and *Due Diligence*

Interior design, Formatting and Indexing
Elyse Gappa

Publisher
Mike French

Special thanks to our "consumer testing group," the dozens of friends who voted, edited and advised on everything from the cover design to the marketing campaign.

Contents

How to Use This Book

It occurred to us as we worked on the content, that tips, traps and secrets are really a lot alike. We felt strongly, however, that readers should be able to scan the book quickly for these items.

What are tips, traps and secrets, anyway?

Tips

Tips are reminders of things you already know, or expansions of your knowledge of a subject or given items. They may be gentle reminders of what should be obvious or just a little idea to help you make something easier or to steer clear of trouble.

Traps

These are what will for sure get you in trouble if you do (or don't do) them. These can be "booger bears," as Ron says. Greg has a fancy banker word for them, but that would be boring, wouldn't it?

Secrets

Secrets are things you may not have known. They may delve into how a banker thinks, or things he does or knows that you didn't know. In most cases, he won't care that you know them – they make you a better customer – but in some cases they may help you minimize costs, which may or may not reduce the banker's profits. Ron emphasizes that he doesn't believe that there are very many real secrets in a bank. Sure, they have backroom discussions just like any company, but in most cases, they are pretty open, and even on items they don't generally jump to disclose, if asked they will tell you. Or tell you that they can't tell you.

Want to know why the banker said no? Ask. A good banker will tell you, they aren't shy. If they won't, you are at the wrong bank. Or they may be required by law not to tell you, as it involves an investigation or other action within or from outside the bank, but they can't reveal it. Many of the "secrets" aren't secrets at all; the authors learned them with years of experience and by reading to learn more about banking. That doesn't mean you shouldn't want to learn them – and quickly – rather than learning them through the school of hard knocks.

❖ ❖ ❖ ❖ ❖

Chapter 1

All I Need is Money

If you ask most people what their greatest business need is, they'll answer "money." Whether that business has been around for a few years, is a start-up venture or is still a plan written on a scrap of paper, many entrepreneurs believe that the only thing holding them back is a bigger supply of money.

That's probably the furthest thing from the truth. If you give a struggling business more money, **chances are good that all it's going to do is lose more money.** Why? Because that business hasn't figured out what its true business issues are. The owner hasn't taken the time to address the genuine problems facing his or her business — so more money is only going to feed those problems.

TRAP!

The truth is, there is plenty of money in the world today. Banks are sitting on money, investors are sitting on money and individuals are sitting on money, all waiting for the right opportunity to put that money to work. And while there are millions of ideas for businesses out there, very few people can take those ideas, connect them with the money and turn them into successful ventures.

Lesson No. 1: Know What You Need – And Why You Need It.

Greg: As a banker, I constantly see people who think all they need is more money. For example, I had a prospect who came into the bank who owned an ice cream store. He and his buddy had gone into business together and each of them had put in $100,000, and now they're both broke and don't know what to do. They were delinquent on payroll, owed back taxes and had no business plan. A business plan needs to be clearly articulated, to include directions how one will reach their vision. Dreams don't have directions.

What he did have was a **big pile of receipts** — a pretty good sign that he didn't know where he had been or where he was going. He was completely blind. He thought they had a competitive advantage with this ice cream they were selling, but he hadn't even thought about how many scoops of ice cream he had to sell just to pay to finish out his building! If you can't put your competitive advantage into numbers, is it really a competitive advantage?

You have to know how much money you need now. You have to know why you need it. And you have to know how much you're going to need going forward.

Ron: So, he hadn't figured out what his metrics were? Metrics are the numerical measurements of performance for a business. The simplest might be sales per month, but many more are needed to understand your business, such as more complex ones like average **client acquisition cost.** (For more information on client acquisition cost, visit Ron's web site and blog, www.MrMissionPossible.com.) Money was the last thing he needed! He needed to find out how he got that tax lien — and what he was going to do differently if they ran short of money.

In [my book] *Green Weenies*, we had a question: "How big is the hole and how are we going to fill it?" In other words, how big is the deficit, and what plan can we devise to erase it? It's an estimate of how much sales or income you'll need to solve the problem. **A lot of people just don't spend enough time** — especially when they're in trouble and even when they're just starting out — trying to understand how big the hole is and how they are going to fill it.

Greg: That's a good point. I asked this prospect, "How much money are you going to lose every month?" and he said, "I don't know that we do lose money every month." He had no idea what his financial statements said.

Ron: Customers who are headed to the bank looking for a loan need to look over their financials and meet with their accountant **to make sure they understand what the numbers mean**. And if you

How big is the hole, and how are we going to fill it? – In other words, how big is the financial deficit and what plan can we devise to erase it? The size of "the hole" is similar to the *burn rate*, but not exactly the same thing. The *burn rate* can be either a current or projected cash depletion rate. The size of "the hole" is an estimate of how much sales, income or cash is needed to solve a problem or potential crisis. Such a hole was likely created by cash depletion or other unexpected event. It can also apply quite nicely to production, shipping and other areas. If you miss production numbers, how big is the hole and how will you fill it? You may have to shift production to another plant.
(See also: *burn rate and runway*.)

Use: "Although the company is quite profitable, the pending asbestos litigation forced everyone to ask *'How big is the hole, and how are we going to fill it?'* "

Illustrations by Gahan Wilson and/or definitions from *Green Weenies* and *Due Diligence* (www.greenweenies.com) by Ron Sturgeon are used throughout the book

don't understand them, you need to bring someone to the bank with you who does!

TIP

If a banker gets a sense that you don't understand the financials, then the **banker wants to know that you have someone credible working for or with you** who does understand them and can give you that information. But to go into a bank and not understand what's going on with your financial statements is a critical mistake.

It's kind of like the guy who comes in and says he wants to buy a Ferrari, but all he's ever driven is a Volkswagen. He doesn't know what a Ferrari can do; he just likes the idea of owning one.

Greg: A lot of people like the idea of having a corner office, a company car and an expense account, but they don't do the work to get there. Many business owners want to improve their circumstances, but they are unwilling to improve themselves.

Getting There Is Half the Fun

TIP

Doing the work to get there means taking the idea from your head and putting it into a solid plan. **It means creating a business plan that is honest and viable and defines your objectives, possible pitfalls and your action plan for making it happen.** What else does it take to create a business plan that will gain your banker's trust and help you get the funding you need?

There are plenty of software programs and books to advise you on what bells and whistles need to be included in your business plan. But when you strip all those away, what is going to make your plan strong enough to succeed?

Lesson No. 2: Becoming the Person with the Plan

Ron: I guess we can overstate the obvious and say the first thing bankers don't want to see is a business plan written on a big yellow pad with a No. 2 pencil…

SECRET

Greg: True, but at the same time I want to know that the person whom I'm dealing with wrote the plan and understands it. When someone brings me a business plan in a fancy folder, **the first thing**

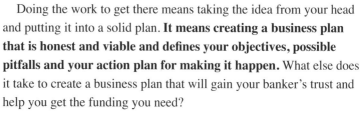

I'm going to do is throw the fancy folder away. If I kept them all, I'd have a stack of plastic folders as high as a skyscraper. Try using a manila folder; they're practical and inexpensive.

Ron: So as a banker, what are you looking for in the business plan?

Greg: The first thing I want to know is what you do, and how you do it better than other people.

SECRET

Ron: I call that a **Unique Selling Proposition (USP)**. When someone tells me they have an idea for a business, one of the first things I ask is, "What's your USP?" And they'll start talking about how their service is going to be better or they're going to have a bigger commitment to quality.

What they don't understand — and what I always tell them — is that those are features, not benefits, and they're not unique! It's hard to define a Unique Selling Proposition. And by the way, I'm not saying that having the best service is a bad USP, but I want them to tell me what makes their service better. What are they willing to do to make their service different from everybody else's? I want to understand that. Good examples of USPs might include:

- Our machine does something the competing machine doesn't do (that's the feature), and that translates into a third less operating expense (that's the benefit).
- We are going to offer better customer service (a feature). We will accomplish that by making sure that the widgets the client requests will actually fill his need (a benefit); our competitors just sell the client what he asks for with no questions asked.
- Our delivery is faster and more accurate (a feature). We accomplish that by using RFID tags attached to the merchandise throughout the distribution process (notice that we discuss exactly how we will accomplish a goal). They will know at every point where the item is, so we and they can identify a problem earlier in the fulfillment process and eliminate disappointment (a benefit). RFID is radio frequency

identification technology; an RFID tag attached to an item reports where the item is for inventory and logistics purposes.

TRAP

Greg: A lot of times, people think being the **lowest-cost provider** is their benefit. But when they say that, it's almost always automatic that I'm not making that loan.

Ron: You almost never want to be the low-cost provider…

Greg: No, you don't! People don't realize that if they underprice their competitors, they're the ones who are going to go away, not their competition. No one wins in a price war. No one! You have to have some kind of benefit that customers are willing to pay a little bit more for. And I'm not talking about having a building with a pretty lobby … you have to have that USP.

Ron: So, from a banker's standpoint, what else do you want to see? You're expecting their business plan to include what they do, a little bit about their background and their successes — but not too much. They need to make it very succinct. Would you say that's correct?

TIP

Greg: Yeah, and I want to know that they have experience doing what they want to do. If they don't, **they need to have a partner that does.** The business plan they give me should basically be their loan write-up. It should give the banker enough information to go in front of the loan committee and say, here's why they need the money. And more importantly, here's how they're going to pay it back. I need to know about your background, I need to know good things about you and I need to know if I'm going to read something bad about you in the paper tomorrow morning.

TIP

Ron: Yes, the days of lending on "ideas" are over. Experience and a track record of success are imperative. About the business plan, on the other hand, you don't want too much information. With most business plans that people give me, they're one of two things — and they're both wrong. **Either they're one or two pages or they're 35 or 40 pages.**

A business plan should be as succinct as possible, but it should also be as complete as possible. It should have the math — the pro forma math for at least three years and maybe as many as five. If this is an existing business and there's a history, it should have some math from that. The banker wants to see how the cash flows, and it should include information about the people, their education, their experience, their product or service and the company.

It needs to have an overview of what they're planning to do and how they're going to use the money. And to address your point, Greg, it should have the primary, secondary and last (gasp, this is a curse word to a banker) source of repayment. The value of the collateral is seen as the weakest source of repayment, because it's almost always impaired at the time of repossession or foreclosure, so make sure there are other sources of repayment rooted in cash. And all of that should run between eight and 20 pages. Many times customers think that they should get a loan because their collateral is good, but that would be asset-based lending. Bankers want the collateral to be the last source of repayment, so if you don't project cash flow, they don't want your loan.

I think you always need to include an executive summary that isn't any longer than four pages and has some excerpts from the math, like charts with the top line and bottom line — a condensed version of the full-blown business plan. That would be my idea of what a banker wants to see.

Greg: That's all good. We also want to see an outline that has the business description, the name of the business, location, a description of products or services, and management expertise. Then it should go into their own business history. How long have they been in business? What does the ownership look like, and what makes them qualified to run this business? And finally, you need to define your business goals and give a financial summary.

If you can put all that together, you are off to a good start.

Putting the Planning Back into Your Business Plan

Having a completed business plan doesn't necessarily make you ready to meet your banker any more than filling out a dating profile on eHarmony.com makes you ready to get married. There are still several steps that need to be taken before you sit down with your banker. Like a first date, these things require time and preparation.

The first step is making sure that your plan isn't just done, but that it's done well. It's vital to know that it can stand up to the scrutiny and questioning it's going to receive at the bank. You don't want to find out that your math is flawed *after* you've given the plan to your banker; this is the time to slow down, kick the tires and make sure your plan is ready to hit the road.

Lesson No. 3 – Taking Your Plan for a Test Drive

SECRET

Greg: People don't understand that one of the most important things they need to do is to **take their business plan to someone else before they take it to the bank and try to get money.** Nine times out of 10, someone else is going to find mistakes, or omissions, and ask appropriate hard questions.

That's the kind of thing they want to hear from someone else, *not* from the banker that they're trying to get money from!

Ron: I think it's imperative to have someone else review a business plan before you take it to the bank. Have two other people go over it, because they might see different things.

But when you give the plan to someone else to review, don't prejudice them. Just give it to them, no explanation, and ask, "What do you think?"

Greg: And whom you give it to is important. It has to be a real friend or a trusted colleague who will tell you what you *need* to hear, not just what you want to hear. It needs to be someone who'll say, "Are you crazy? Why would you even put that in here?!" Of course, that person needs to be qualified to opine on the plan.

TRAP

Ron: One of the problems that I think many people are guilty of when making a business plan is that they start **breathing their own exhaust too much.** They start listening to themselves and thinking about what a great idea they have — and what they need is somebody who will tell them what they really think about that idea.

Unfortunately, there aren't that many people out there who are either willing or qualified to do that. I see a lot of people who say they can help raise money for businesses, and there are people who would be glad to take someone's check, say, for $25,000 in return for some type of proposed stock offering document, but the investor (if one or more can be found) is never going to see any money back from such an investment. Because those people are just telling business persons what they want to hear and helping them breathe their own exhaust so that they can take their money to help with an **offering that never happens**. If a person has a history of success, and a viable concept, **they will attract money, either debt or equity.**

SECRET

Greg: That's one of the reasons it's so important that the person who delivers the business plan be the person who wrote it. Don't have some college kid draw it up; be behind it and know what's in it. It becomes pretty clear pretty quickly if someone has had someone else draw up his or her business plan, because those are the people who can't answer the banker's questions. Also, to make your first meeting more productive, **send the plan and a copy of your tri-bureau credit report at least a few days before your proposed meeting.** Cut though the crap and get right into reviewing it on your first visit. (More on credit reports later.)

TIP

TIP

It's important that the person sitting in front of the banker can answer all of his questions about the business plan.

Ron: One way to make sure you can do this — and I'm not sure that bankers will like this idea, but it works — is for the people seeking the loan to take that business plan to a bank that they know isn't going to give them the loan. Or they can **take it to a bank that they know they don't want to do business with**. The bankers will tell him everything that is wrong with his business plan. Then he can go back and fix all those things, because I can guarantee you that the bank they do want to do business with will have those same concerns. But don't let them pull a credit report on you; that lowers

SECRET

your credit score and lets other lenders know that you may have been turned down by another bank.

So now they've improved their plan, they can take it to the bank they want to do business with and have a better chance of getting a loan.

Greg: Yeah, and here's another way to do that: They should find someone who's in the same industry, but not necessarily in direct competition. They might be across the country and the person needing the help is never going to run into them or compete directly with them.

That's the kind of person to take the business plan to and say, "Here's the package that I'm going to take to the bank. Can you tell me what you think of it?" The other person might have a bigger business, might be smaller; maybe they've been a mentor for a while. The bottom line is that it's not going to cost anything, and because it's not a direct competitor, the businessperson isn't going to lose any kind of competitive advantage by turning it over to the other person.

Ron: I do a lot of small-business consulting, and much of that involves people who are trying to start a business. Normally, I'll charge them about $5,000 to work through their plans and processes and help them with all of that. Obviously, the scope can grow a lot bigger and become more expensive, or sometimes it ends up costing less because, once we get into it, they realize this is something they shouldn't even consider doing.

It's important to have someone else's help. There are plenty of consultants out there — and no, I'm not talking about somebody who is just going to help raise money. I mean a true business consultant, who for a few thousand dollars will go through the plan and find all the stuff that doesn't make sense. These are the people who may not necessarily be smarter than you on the math, but who have seen lots of business plans. They understand them. I use a lot of consultants to help me, and the cost up front is well worth it. Most of the time, the person says, or thinks, that they can't afford that help, which is a huge mistake. They can't afford to *not* get that help.

Whenever people create a business plan, I tell them to figure that it's going to take twice as long, be twice as expensive and, in the end, they'll end up being about half right. They need to find someone who can work with them to help them figure that all out.

When Bad Plans Happen to Good People

Even the best business ideas can be sidelined by a bad business plan. Knowing what a banker is looking for is one of the best ways to keep it from going straight into the trash. But it also needs to be solid and realistic. It needs to be thorough enough for the banker to be able to write a loan package from its details.

That means including why you need the money — and how you plan to pay it back. Keep in mind that banks lend money because they expect to get a return on it, so establishing a plan for paying it back is paramount.

Lesson No. 4 – Covering the Bases from the Bottom Up

TIP

Ron: One thing that I like to do, and I know most people don't do it that much, is called **bottom-up planning**. These days, it's really easy to create a spreadsheet and create a top line where advertising costs are five percent, labor is 20 percent and so forth.

But what about the metrics? Like with the ice cream shop: how many scoops of ice cream are they going to sell? Once they've figured that out, they need to extrapolate that into how many cups and cones they'll need to buy, how many freezers they'll need, how many employees they'll need to scoop all that ice cream. And if they're going to sell 10,000 scoops a day, how many tables will they need, and how big will their lobby need to be to hold all those people, and how big a parking lot it would take to accommodate all those cars.

TIP

I would say that 98 percent of the business plans I see haven't been looked at that way. Also, a **bridge plan is needed for yourself, and the highlights for your banker.** Visit my site (www.MrMissionPossible.com) for more information on bridge plans and bottom up planning.

Greg: That's a problem we see a lot. I know of a couple of brothers from a foreign country who wanted to open a restaurant in a small town. When they opened a checking account at a local bank, the banker told them that in order to be successful, they needed to be able to make a great chicken fried steak. When they left the bank, the brothers asked each other, "What's a chicken fried steak?"

Ron: And it's not just new businesses. Once I was in a bank and overheard a conversation in the next booth. The guy sold parts and provided services for 1964 through 1966 Ford Mustangs, and he'd been doing this for several years. He'd been blindsided because all of a sudden his business had slowed down.

All I could think was, "How stupid is that?!" There are a finite number of 1966-1968 Mustangs, and how many people are out there to fix them? He hadn't thought to expand into servicing modern Mustangs, or adding Camaros or some other car. So now he was in the bank trying to get a loan to get out of this bad situation he was in.

TRAP

He had obviously been very **unstrategic in his planning**, and the banker had to be concerned about how he got there. I mean, who couldn't see that coming? What does that mean, unstrategic in planning? It means that you think about what may happen, and then what happens as a result of that, good and bad, think about all scenarios. Beef up your plan accordingly, but you will also **be prepared when the banker asks "but what if that happens?"**

TIP

Greg: Sounds like that customer was trying to become the eight-track player of his industry. One of the problems we see a lot is that people are managing for the quarter, not for the quarter century.

Ron: That's how they end up with "green weenies" in the business plan. A green weenie is exactly what it sounds like — a weenie that's been left in the refrigerator for three months with the refrigerator unplugged … you might call it a very unpleasant surprise. A banker doesn't want any of those.

And they aren't there to give advice. I am amazed at the bankers who've told me stories about a customer who comes in and says,

Green Weenie – The disgusting term that started my word quest. When I first heard *"green weenie,"* I realized there was another language being spoken in the business world with mysterious words and acronyms, some funny ha-ha, some funny weird, some just wacky, some with hidden meanings and some downright offensive. Imagine what a weenie must look like when it is left in a refrigerator (which is unplugged) and forgotten for six months. A *green weenie* in business wheeling and dealing lingo is an unpleasant surprise discovered belatedly as part of a transaction or deal. If you discover at the end of your negotiations with a distributor that your would-be supplier was in bankruptcy a year ago, that's a green weenie. If, during your due diligence, you discover that the receivables are much older than expected or that the revenues are recognized on an accounting basis that is unacceptable to the IRS, those are green weenies. The image calls to mind something that would likely cause food poisoning. *Green Weenie* is also the nickname of a Pittsburgh Pirates magic charm icon used to put hexes on opposing teams.

Use: "Chip learned three days before closing a merger that a huge delayed order of dealer returns was expected to arrive at the merger partner's warehouse two weeks after consummating the merger, resulting in a post-closing write-off. That *green weenie* could kill the deal."

"I need some money but I'm not really sure how much. How much do you think I'm going to need?" That banker is absolutely not interested in giving them any advice — and probably won't lend them any money! I am always amazed at the borrowers who ask the banker how much do they need. Isn't that silly?

Greg: Another thing we don't want to see is three years' worth of monthly historical financials. When someone brings us a business proposal with thousands of numbers in it, we get lost. Bring us annual or, at the most, quarterly statements. I don't usually need to see monthly statements.

Ron: But as an entrepreneur, I need to know what those monthly numbers are!

Greg: Sure, business owners need monthly numbers to figure out how they're going to hit their projections. **Because if you can't measure it, you can't manage it.**

So gather your monthly numbers (metrics), but **don't think that the banker wants to see all of that.** Too much data just drowns them, or triggers unnecessary concerns and anxiety for all. Not gathering monthly numbers is like playing a basketball game with the scoreboard covered up, then pulling the cover off at the end of the game to see which team won, without understanding the strategies, failures, and successes of the game. To a banker, numbers talk.

Ron: There are a lot of people who say that business plans are crap; they're not really needed, they're way too much work. I was guilty of that in my early years. But those people will never be as successful as they'd like. It's hard work and it's a lot of planning, but it's not just for the bank, **a business plan is so much more, and should be the road map you are executing against, measuring your success and making course corrections.**

Greg: Right. Every company needs to have its own strategic plan. If someone has a goal and it's not in writing, then it's just a dream. As I said before, dreams don't have a direction.

Ron: What else do bankers want to see? **You want to see some**

skin in the game, right? What does that mean in terms of down payments and equity and those kinds of things?

Greg: Never go in and ask a bank for 100 percent financing on anything. I want the customer to have some skin in the game; maybe put down 20 percent on whatever it is he or she needs.

Let's say someone comes to the bank and wants to finance a new bulldozer. The day it's driven off the lot, it's not worth the $100,000 it cost, it's worth $80,000. As a banker, I'm already down to having something that is only worth what I just financed. And if the customer has some skin in the game, I know they're going to lose some money if they have that bulldozer taken away.

TRAP

Ron: One of the things I see often in business plans is that the **owners include a big salary for themselves.** People have to live, but I always advise people that before they go to the bank, they reduce their lifestyle to something more modest. And **don't go into the bank with a big credit card debt (unless you have a legitimate reason to have it).** They will see that and instantly think about the lifestyle and discipline it must indicate. In most cases, they need to demonstrate to the banker that they've taken a haircut — they've reduced their wages to do this — which again is showing they have some skin in the game. I don't expect them to work for free, but if they're showing me a business plan where they're paying themselves $200,000 a year, and they're going to lose $200,000 in that first year, I'm going to ask them why they don't pay themselves $75,000 and only lose $125,000 that first year.

TIP

Greg: And let's go back to the down payment idea for a moment. The more you put down, the less your interest expense is. The first thing I ask people when someone comes in looking for money is, "Why haven't you paid off your cars?" They might have $100,000 in the bank, and they owe $20,000 on a car. Why not pay off the car loan and avoid paying the interest?

TIP

If a banker wants you to put 20 percent down, and you have the money to put 25 percent down and are willing to put it down, that banker is going to really think favorably about your request.

Ron: How do you feel about how fast a company can grow and what they should show in their business plan? Typically, people tend to over-forecast.

Greg: A lot of the business plans we get are hilarious. People think they're going to become millionaires overnight. We'll get pro formas that show they're going to bring in a million dollars in revenue in their first month. I don't know many companies that can do that.

Another thing people do on their pro formas is leave off the interest expense. Hello? They're in a bank asking for money! Aren't they going to pay me back? They have rental expenses for their warehouse space, but no rental expense for the money they want to borrow! Another common omission is . If someone is going to make money, doesn't it make sense that they're going to be taxed on those profits?

Ron: I always tell people that bankers always ask for profit and loss statements, either quarterly or annually. Banks aren't interested in a 28-page profit and loss (P&L) statement. They want to see the big expense items like the cost of goods and labor, and they want to see general and administrative costs. They might ask for some details, and a business needs to know those things if they do, but the bank is not that interested in all the details. It's a little more work to boil it down, **but one page is enough for a P&L.** Condense all the smaller details, leaving material items shown, into what's called a compiled statement. Your banker doesn't care if your cleaning service charges $200 per month, when your monthly expenses total $75,000.

I'm amazed at what people will send to a bank. **Never, ever send something to a bank without looking at it.** Go over the numbers, see what they mean and think about it. As a business owner, I have to know and understand everything I provide to the bank.

Greg: Another important thing to do is **put those annual or quarterly statements side by side and compare them.** Any change of more than, say, five or 10 percent should be explained. Any kind of variance in revenue or profit needs to be explained. The bank is going to want to know why that changed, and if the customer doesn't know, how can he or she expect the banker to explain it to the loan committee? Bankers are big on variances, good or bad.

Ron: From an entrepreneur's aspect, I have a different attitude. We know that most bankers are not going to study what I've given them, so I'm not going to show my banker all those changes.

If it's all good, I'll include that information and point it out. **But if one of my expenses is bigger than it should be, I'll put it in "general and administrative expenses" and won't point it out.** I've found that well over half of bankers don't compare this stuff year after year, so I don't see it as being critical. But don't let that dissuade you from doing it for your own planning. You *should* compare the statements. And understand the differences. You are so dead if the banker does it and you don't have an instant explanation, one including any required solutions. Bankers love candor, and they especially love someone that is *on it*, in control and that understands all the nuances of their business. You will be a great customer if you do this work – or have it done, but be *on it*.

Ready, Set, Grow…

Growth is a part of every successful business. In business plans, that anticipated growth is often wildly overstated. But too much growth is just as hazardous as no growth at all.

While many new business owners think that rapid growth is the ideal scenario, growth that occurs too quickly can result in the exact opposite. Nobody expects an infant to grow to adulthood in a year; it's not healthy for a business to grow that rapidly, either. Knowing how much you can realistically expect your business to grow is key in creating a plan.

Lesson No. 5 – Preparing (and Projecting) for Growth

Ron: One of the things a banker doesn't want to see in a business plan is unrealistic growth rates.

Greg: Absolutely. You can kill yourself by growing too fast, and most people don't realize that.

SECRET

Ron: It's called a hockey stick. It's an unrealistic change in the numbers, usually growing too fast. **Borrowers actually think big growth will impress a lender and increase their chance of getting a loan.** Nothing could be farther from the truth.

Monthly Sales

Example of a Hockey Stick

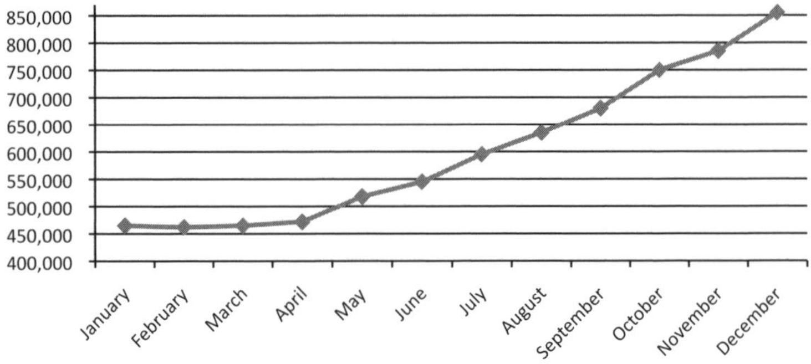

Greg: Right. And if a business' revenue is going up too fast, the owners have to bring in more inventory to meet demand, and so their receivables are increasing — there's not a chance for them to repay that loan in the short run.

TIP

Ron: Revenue going up is not the same as profit going up. **People need to understand the cash flow and where the money goes.** If receivables double, the company needs the cash to fund that. That means if receivables went from $100,000 to $200,000, the company needs an additional $100,000. And there are three ways to get that:

SECRET

One, they can write a check to the company, which would likely be capital. (It can **also be structured for tax reasons as a note payable to the shareholder,** but the bank may want it subordinated to the bank's debt.) Two, they can get a loan for $100,000; or three, they can produce $100,000 worth of profit that isn't needed elsewhere to fund the growth. On a startup, the profit source is the most unlikely.

Too often, people don't understand cash flow, so they don't understand that issue. But the bottom line is, bankers don't want to see hockey sticks in business plans. And your **loan request is going to be DOA** if you don't anticipate and plan for the required amount of cash needed, whether from debt, profits, or equity.

TRAP:

Greg: There's a huge difference between revenue and income. Revenue is the dollars coming in; income is what's left after all the expenses. A lot of people refer to revenue as income.

Ron: So from a banker's point of view, what is a quantifiable number that people can look at in a business plan when talking about growth?

Greg: If they have projected anything over a 10 percent growth rate, they're going to need to explain it. Twenty-five percent growth will often kill a company.

Ron: That's for a mature business, right? Because for a start-up, it's easy to double $10,000 sales to $20,000.

Greg: Sure, it's easy for a start-up business to show rapid growth in the beginning, because of where it's starting out. But that kind of growth most likely won't continue. And a business plan shouldn't project that a start-up would continue growing at an exorbitant pace. But even in start ups, I want to believe that the growth is founded in good metrics. **When a loan request shows doubling of sales, and production, I want to know where the doubled rent is for the warehouse.** I hope the answer is faster inventory turns, if the prospect didn't show increased rent.

TIP

What Bankers Want

One important component in creating a business plan is knowing what bankers want, and don't want, to see in it. Knowing those expectations not only helps you prepare a better business plan, but it makes the meeting easier for both of you.

Lesson No. 6 – Giving Your Banker What They Want

Ron: I always tell people that they have to be prepared to lift the kimono a little bit, which means letting the banker look in. They need to be prepared to explain to [the banker] what's under there.

Greg: People get concerned about doing that, but banks have rules that prohibit them from telling others what they have seen under your kimono. Bankers can be fired very easily for having loose lips.

Ron: The banker doesn't want to hear SWAGs or WAGs. A SWAG is a Scientific Wild-Ass Guess and a WAG is a Wild-Ass Guess.

TIP

The banker doesn't want to hear that someone needs a loan because the economy is bad or they're getting a divorce or the weather's been bad. The banker needs to hear legitimate reasons why business is down or off. Along with solutions.

In a declining market, the businessperson has to figure out how to work harder or smarter to keep the business going. Most people keep doing what they've been doing, so they keep getting what they've been getting or worse.

Greg: That's a good point. Do not go into a bank whining about the economy. A banker should know if the economy is bad; but when a customer comes in and is all gloom and doom … the banker doesn't want to hear it. If there's a problem, I want to know about it, but don't come in just to tell me how bad the economy is.

TIP

I also want to know that customers are beating the street. I want them to have an air of confidence about their plans. That's going to go a long way. And don't confuse confidence with arrogance.

Ron: You want them to come in with solutions, not problems! My old boss at Ford Motor Co., Dixon Thayer, liked to say he was

positively dissatisfied with results. He was all about positive energy, but knew we could do more.

TIP

Greg: Exactly. Show me the baby, not the labor pains. That's what I want to see.

TIP

Ron: The banker also likes to see business owners who **surround themselves with people who are smarter or better than** they are, and or that will do things that you can't, won't or shouldn't be doing. If you arent good at financials, get someone that is. It's important to show that there are good people on your team. I can not emphasize the importance of this enough!

For example, there was a time when I realized (after much hand wringing, as I was so frugal) I should quit paying a bookkeeper and spend the extra money to hire a controller. I went from paying a *bookkeeper* $40,000 a year to paying a *controller* $75,000 a year, but our company made the entire $35,000 back in less than 60 days because he isolated and identified expenses we could cut.

Every Good Business Plan Should Include...

- Name of Business
- Executive summary
- Location
- Ownership information/Brief history of the business/Target markets
- Information on the product/services
- Competition/Environment
- Goals/Strategies
- Financial summary for three years and the latest quarter
- Budgets or pro formas
- Metrics highlights
- Information on the owners and operators, including their track records

What's a pro forma financial statement?

It's a hypothetical or projected, or recast financial statement

TIP

based on forecasted or estimated numbers. Forecasting can be so hard. Ron says that if you **figure in twice as much time and twice as much money as you think you need, you might be safe.** But entrepreneurs seem to always "breathe their own exhaust," and they become infatuated with their own ideas. That's why it's so important to have someone else that is capable to review your plans. You need someone who is willing to tell you how it is (not what you want to hear).

Chapter 2

How to Choose (and Court) a Banker

Most people won't start looking for a banker until they need money, which is a lot like looking for a spouse when you decide you're ready to start a family. Finding the banker who is right for you takes a lot more time and planning than most people realize, and it's something that should be done long before you think you're going to need one.

Banking isn't an event that happens spontaneously; rather, it's a process that needs to be approached carefully and strategically. The first, and probably most important, step is to create a relationship that opens the door for the banking process. Greg advises doing all of your banking in person so that you can get to know more of the people at the bank. Ron adds that this is perhaps impractical for many business owners, but you do have to *know* your banker and the staff. Make sure that when feasible, you *don't* use the drive through for deposits, go in. **Stop and say hi at least once monthly, perhaps while cashing a check.**

TIP

But before you do that, you'll need to **spend some time researching the banks that are accessible to you and finding out which ones would best meet your needs. In Ron's book, *Green Weenies* and *Due Diligence,* it's called a "beauty contest."** It means you're going to size up the competition and see which one looks the best to you. But don't worry — this doesn't mean that you'll have to see your banker in a swimsuit competition.

SECRET

Lesson No. 1 – Looking for the Right Banker

Greg: Banks are like doctors. They specialize in different things. If your hand hurts, you're not going to go to a heart doctor. If you have a brain tumor, you see a neurosurgeon. Banks are the same way. If you're a businessperson, you need to find a business bank, not a consumer bank. For example, you don't want to go to a credit union if you're looking for a business loan, because they specialize in consumers. **You need to look at what your needs are and what that bank provides. Don't try to fool a banker, they've seen it all, and know it when they see *all hat and no cattle*.**

TIP

You also need to look at whether you need a big national chain or a local bank. If you have 100 locations, maybe it's important for you to have a chain that can serve you in a lot of locations. But if you have a single location, maybe you would be better off with a local bank. You need a bank where you can go in, state your case and have the person across the table be able to make a decision. And if it's for your business, you need to make sure that it's a business bank. You have to find a bank that does what you do.

Ron: Personally, I think that all banks are greedy. Any bank that you call up and say, "I want to finance a car" or "I want to finance some equipment or get a loan for my company" — they'll all say yes. **I don't think everyone knows whether a bank is a consumer bank or a business bank, so how do people find out?**

SECRET

Greg: You should be able to find that on the bank's web site. Most banks' web sites will tell you what the bank does. They'll have some catchy lines and slogans that don't really say anything; you have to go through all that and make sure that the bank can do what you need it to be able to do.

Ron: Once you've found the bank you want to do business with, how do you choose whom in the bank to talk to? **All of the people on the lower floor of the bank are called "relationship bankers," which is a b.s. term, but it impresses people.** Anyone who walks in or calls the bank without knowing who they are going to meet is going to be paired with a "relationship banker." All that means is that he or she is going to be dealing with someone at a very low level, who is very young, has a very low loan-lending limit and makes decisions based on very black-and-white numbers.

SECRET

All hat, no cattle – Someone who acts like a big shot but has no substance or power or clout; also, someone who acts rich but has no assets. This type of person wants everyone to believe they are talented and can really do the job, but it soon becomes obvious that they can't. As they say in Texas "good ol' boy" business circles: "It's easy to get a hat but much harder to get a herd of cattle." (See also: *empty shirt*.)

Use: "Joe, the new CEO, drops celebrity names like he knows everybody in New York, but he proved to be *all hat, no cattle* when it came to getting us any PR with all his friends in New York."

TIP

Greg: Walking in the door is exactly the wrong thing to do. **A better way is to find out where someone else banks and get them to refer you.**

TIP

Ron: Instead of just getting a referral, **I would even ask them to call the bank as a sounding board and open the door a little bit.** You know, maybe they call up and say, "I have a friend who's a car dealer, and he's looking for a loan, but I wasn't sure if you guys did loans for car dealers."

Greg: That's a good idea. I'm also big on choosing someone who has common interests with you. It might be hunting or fishing or golf; whatever it might be, it helps to have some common ground.

Ron: What about experience? What kind of banking experience should they have?

TRAP

Greg: They should have been a banker for at least five years. But you don't want them to have too much experience, either. If you're planning for the quarter century, not the quarter, you need a banker who's going to be around for a while. You don't want someone who's too young and green, and **you don't want someone who's about to retire.**

SECRET

Ron: You also definitely want to **understand the bank's loan-to-deposit ratio.** Say a bank has $20 million to loan, and it's only loaned out $10 million. That means it has a 50 percent loan-to-deposit ratio. Banks don't make money by not loaning out their money. So then they loan the other half to the Federal Reserve or to someone else at a low rate. But they sometimes only make below 1 percent at the Federal Reserve.

SECRET

SECRET

On the other hand, if a bank has $100 million to loan, but it has loaned out $110 million, it has too many loans for its deposit base. **A bank with a loan-to-deposit ratio of less than about 70 to 75 percent probably wants to make more loans.** But after 90 percent, it probably doesn't. So, as a banker, what would you say is the loan-to-deposit ratio potential customers should look for? All **banks have a legal loan limit**; it's the most they can lend any one client. If your loan is big, ASK, there is no reason to discuss a loan that is too big for the lender. Also, since bankers are greedy (arent most of us?), **they will consider a loan larger than their limit.** They accommodate it by selling off part of it to another bank, **it's called a participation**. You should really try to avoid this, as then you have another lender looking at your stuff, making requests. The original bank will manage the relationship, and wants you to believe it doesn't matter, but don't kid yourself, they have to field requests from the other lender about your relationship, and that means you will have more oversight and paperwork.

SECRET

TRAP

Greg: I would say that a good sweet spot is between a 70 and a 90 percent loan to value ratio. That way, you know they're in the lending business, but they aren't loaned out. Once you go over 70 percent, you know they're in the business of lending money.

Courting Your Banker

Long before asking for money, customers need to begin building a relationship with their bank. They can start by opening a business checking account and getting to know everybody at the bank, but — particularly if it's a new business — don't simply walk into a bank with a business plan and try to borrow some money.

The first step is to decide where you'd like to take your business. Once you've identified the "who," it's time to work on meeting your banker and developing a relationship. If you've done your research, you'll know that this bank is right for you and your business, and you'll also know that the banker has the lending power and is friendly toward your type of business.

If a friend referred the banker to you, one of the best ways to move the relationship forward is to have your friend arrange a lunch meeting with the banker. While your first meeting with the banker should be on your "home turf," a friendly introduction over lunch is an effective way to launch a lasting relationship.

"It's a good idea just to swing by the bank, pick him up — make it easy on the banker," Greg says. **"Lunches are important to**

TIP

bankers. We've got to eat every day, so we might as well make it count."

And you can even get your banker to pick up the check.

Lesson No. 2 – Creating a Relationship With a Banker

Greg: People today really don't put enough time and thought into picking their banker. Picking a banker is kind of like getting married and having kids together — the business owner has to have confidence that the banker is going to lend him or her money, and the bank has to have confidence that the owner is going to pay it back.

If I'm calling on you as a customer, I want my first call to be on your turf. I want to see what you have in your office that's important to you. That way, I know a little bit about your background. In banking, one thing we look at is character. One of the first things I want to find out is what color hat you're wearing — is it a white hat or a black hat?

Ron: I think it's very important that the first meeting occurs at the customer's place of business. I had one deal some years back where a fancy lender came to my place of business. When he got there, he wanted to walk all the way to the back. And I mean all the way to the back. I said, "I don't understand," and he said, **"All the crap is in the back of the building."**

SECRET

He explained that if he was going to finance a warehouse, the first place he'd want to look is in the back of the building, because that's where they're going to store or dump everything, and it's the last place to be cleaned, but can be an indication of "business housekeeping". So basically it's great that you cleaned the glass door and you have all your employees standing at attention, but he wants to go to the back, because that's where you're going to hide all your crap. Murphy's Law says that if you clean it, the banker won't go there. But that's strategic thinking on your part. And remember, no one likes Green Weenies.

Greg: Right. And you want your banker to know and understand what you do, because he or she might be able to help.

SECRET

Ron: I call that meeting stage the champagne phase and I always caution everybody because it really sucks. We clink our glasses and talk about how great this is going to be. The loan officer usually talks like, "This is the deal we're going to do, we're going to give you a great rate and this is going to be great!" And you'll come away from the meeting thinking that everything is going to be okay.

But usually it's not okay; it's just that the crap hasn't hit the fan yet. Because the next thing you know, the bank's going to want lots of stuff from you — lots of documentation you don't have — and the banker's going to ask you questions that you can't answer. Before long it's going to get a lot harder and it's not going to be champagne anymore. By the way, you should have all of that stuff if you're prepared. When I take consulting clients to the bank, or get them ready to go, we provide the banker with virtually everything he could need in advance, then we can forego all of the formalities of going through the plan – which is boring as heck. **We send it via email a few days before (at least 24 hours),** and then when we meet we are just fielding the lender's questions. It makes the meeting very productive.

SECRET

Greg: I call that the "Quixotic phase." It's where everyone is looking at each other with stars in their eyes. Both sides are romantically idealistic. Everyone thinks they're going to get what they want. But that's not going to last.

Meeting the Family

As with any courtship, it won't be long until the relationship needs to involve more than the primary two participants. Meeting other important players at the bank is vital to a successful banking relationship.

A good banker will encourage customers to meet other employees at the bank, from the tellers to other officers. A good customer will take the initiative to build relationships with those employees. That's one reason that most meetings with your banker should be face to face — and, with the exception of that initial meeting, they should be held in the banker's office as often as possible. That gives the customer additional opportunities to establish relationships with a wide range of bank employees.

Another reason to do most of your banking in person? It's a lot easier to tell someone "no" over the phone than it is to tell him or her face to face.

Lesson No. 3 – Expanding Your Banking Relationships

Greg: You also want to know more folks at the bank than just your loan officer. You want to know some people in management. Don't just know your banker; get to know your banker's boss.

Ron: The chief credit officer is another person you should always get to know.

Greg: You need to have a lot of relationships within your bank. Otherwise, if your banker dies or gets hit by a truck or moves away, you're back to square one. **If you're not dealing with the vice president or above, you are probably dealing with the wrong person.** But don't treat that person badly; you just need to create more relationships within the bank to get to the right person. It's important to treat the tellers and secretaries with respect. They've got the ear of the people you need to do business with, and if you don't treat them right, you aren't going to get anywhere. Just like your staff talks about clients, regardless of the appropriateness of that, the **bank staff talks about their clients.** If you are gruff and unsociable, it's going to color all decisions about your relationship. Work on *making* people like you and *want* to help you. Make them look good. They will make you look good, and in the end everyone looks good.

Ron: That's something to keep in mind. You want to meet the people there — the lending officer, the credit officer, and all the other officers you can. And you have to know that you're comfortable with the way they're going to treat you.

The classiest banker I ever knew was a guy named Jim Murray, who worked at Summit Bank. When I met with him, we always sat at the round table in his office. He never met with me from behind his desk. He's the only banker I've ever known who did that.

It goes back to the relationship. It was a philosophy of his, I guess. Because typically the banker sits behind his desk to meet with people and some bankers, I think, use that as a kind of intimidating factor.

SECRET

Greg: They absolutely do. In fact, years ago, banks kept the **bankers' desks elevated so the banker would always be looking down at the customer**. It's a small, subtle thing, but it was intimidating.

TIP

Ron: My point is, Jim had a good bedside manner. It's **important to have someone like that on your side.** On the other hand, I once had a banker introduce me to The Golden Rule: He said that since he had the gold, he'd make the rules. That's not the kind of relationship you want.

I once knew a guy on the board of directors of a bank I was doing business with, and every time my loans came up, he just beat my loan application and my ass. He didn't like me; he didn't like my loans; he didn't like my business. **Finally, the loan officer whom I knew at the bank let me know that this same guy always questioned my loans.**

SECRET

So I asked my loan officer to set up a meeting. The loan officers brought him out and we all went to lunch together. After that, he was my biggest advocate. Once he realized that I knew my business and knew what I was doing, he liked me. It changed my entire relationship with that bank.

Does Size Matter?

Today, customers have a wide range of banks to choose from. Doing some online research before making your selection is imperative, because you don't want to waste your time pursuing an institution that's not right for you. Customers need to not only make sure that they are pursuing a relationship with a bank that understands their business, but also that they are dealing with a bank that can meet their financial needs.

Lesson No. 4 – One Size Does Not Fit All

TIP

SECRET

Ron: I'm a huge advocate of community banks. With big banks, if you can fit in their box, you're fine. Everyone thinks, well, I have a checking account at My Big Bank; I financed my car there, so I'm going to go see them about my business loan. But generally speaking, the underwriting policies at big banks are **not going to give you credit for your experience;** they're not going to give you credit for your character. You need to be at a community bank.

Greg: You need to have a bank that matches your business philosophy and the size of your business. You simply have to have the bank that matches you. Sometimes, it's not about scale; it's about skill.

You don't need a big bank if you're a little widget manufacturer. Now, if you're an international widget manufacturer, then you might need an international bank. But for most people, that's not the case. So you need to find a bank that is the right size for you.

SECRET

TRAP

Ron: It's also important to know the size of the bank, because that could have a lot to do with its appetite for lending. And you want to know what your individual **lender's loan authority** is before you make that decision. I used to ask people that straight out. Some people would tell me; others would dance around it. **But when a lender tells me his loan authority is $25,000, I know I'm meeting with the wrong person.**

SECRET

Every lender has a "choke point." Some lenders can make a loan of up to $300,000 with no problem, but when it gets above that, they start sweating. And when it gets above $500,000, they choke. It might be a wonderful loan, but they just have a threshold that they can't get past.

It doesn't make them bad loan officers. But it does limit your ability to grow, so if you happen to be with an officer like that, and you need to go beyond his or her choke point, you're going to have wasted time building a relationship only to find your lender isn't able to grow with you past this point.

You also want to consider the process for loan approval relative to loan authority. All of the banks have different ways of handling this. Some of the banks layer these amounts so if you have a loan for $100,000, another officer can make a loan for $100,000 and then a third guy can make a loan for $100,000, so together they can make a $300,000 loan, without board approval. Just ask, most will tell you what their process is.

Other banks will give you $100,000 and then once you go past that, it goes to a committee, up to a million dollars. At $1 million it goes to a senior committee, and then at $5 million it goes to the board. The numbers may be different, but you get the picture.

SECRET

Every bank has its own procedures, so you'll need to learn those. Ask, they will usually tell you the amounts and the processes.

Ideally, you'll find a loan officer who can work with you. But it's not the amount of the loan that's important; it's the size of the debt. Say you get with an officer and his authority is $100,000, and you borrow that amount. Then the next day you need to borrow $5,000. **Well, now you're in big trouble because you have to go to the next concurrence officer or go through the next level of approval.** So you have to know going into it how much authority they have. I can recall an instance where I owed $992,000, and wanted to finance a forklift costing $25,000. Because I passed the threshold of $1,000,000, a whole new underwriting process kicked in for all my credit, not just the forklift loan.

TRAP

Greg: And those numbers have changed drastically. At one point, I had a $2 million loan limit. But those were different times. What I would say is that they need to have a loan officer with at least a $100,000 loan limit.

Ron: This is one of those cases, I guess, where you don't necessarily know what the right number is, but you definitely know when it's a wrong number. And $25,000 would be the wrong number. Because that indicates right off the bat that the loan officer is possibly brand new and doesn't know the ropes, and that the bank doesn't have a lot of confidence in his or her ability yet.

Cheating On Your Banker

Having a good bank that you can rely on is important for every business and businessperson. But even though it's important to create an ongoing, solid relationship with that lender, it's also important to have a second bank that you can turn to.

TIP

A second bank gives customers the option of accessing money that the first bank might not be willing to loan. In today's banking climate, with all banks being more hesitant to make loans, it's more important than ever to create relationships with more than one bank. From the bank's standpoint, your primary bank is the one that has your primary checking account; you'll want to use the same diligence in selecting a secondary bank as you followed to find your primary bank.

TIP

It's important to note that **having a second bank isn't about being able to shave another quarter of a percentage point off a loan rate;** it's about being able to get what's best for you and your business. And at the same time, you'll find that when banks are competing for your business, you're more likely to get the best rates available. But you don't have to promote the competition; they KNOW the other bank is out there. If you have credibility, they will generally price you without your having to ask for a deal.

Lesson No. 5 – Getting What You Want, How You Want It

Ron: Once I have an established relationship with a bank, I can take my loan to one lender and let him or her look at it. Then, if I don't get the rate I want, I can go show it to somebody else. But I'm not doing that over something as small as a quarter point; that's not a good enough reason to shop a loan and banks hate people who fight over a quarter point. If you weren't going to be able to make the payment at 7.5 percent, it's not going to make much difference to go to 7.25 percent!

Greg: A lot of it, too, has to do with having a more mature company. When you're more established, you're in a better position to shop a loan around to more than one bank.

Ron: I have a really good example of how having more than one bank works and why it makes sense: In my early years in business, we had a junkyard and we used to pull the engines out of junked vehicles with what was called a pole truck. It looked like a wrecker, except that it had a long pole with a winch at the end that would let you lift the car up and get underneath it to take it apart.

Someone mentioned that using a forklift would make the job a lot easier. So I went to the bank and said I wanted a loan to buy a forklift. I explained what I wanted to do — using a forklift like that was kind of a new idea at the time — and how it would help my business.

Well, the banker didn't agree. He gave me a big bunch of crap about it and told me I didn't need a forklift. This is one of the problems that businesspeople run into. Bankers shouldn't be interested in how you run your business. If you do have a banker who's that concerned about how you're running your business, and you're getting good results, then you have the wrong banker.

Anyway, my banker finally did finance the forklift — and it was wonderful! It was such an innovation for our business and it was saving us time and money, so within a few months I wanted another forklift.

I went back to the bank and my banker said, 'Well, what the hell, Ron? We just financed one forklift!" He wouldn't do it. Even though it was good for my business and was saving my company money, he wouldn't do it.

So I went to another bank and got the loan. They didn't know I already had a forklift, and weren't concerned about anything except my ability to repay. And today, with the banking system so seized up, I would say it's even more important. The bottom line is that you need more than one bank. The bankers may not like it, but it's a reality.

TIP

Greg: That also keeps the **two banks honest from a price standpoint.** If I know that Ron can go to his other bank, it's going to keep me honest. The right bank wants you to do well, and you should want your bank to do well so it can stay in business.

TIP

TRAP

Ron: And you should keep in mind that this isn't just about getting a little bit shaved off your loan rate. I don't want to be that type of guy, and nobody else should be, either. I want to be the guy that, when I walk through the doors, the banker points at me and says, **"We make a lot of money off that guy and he is a really good customer."** If you're the guy who is always busy trying to save a quarter point, you're never going to have that kind of relationship with your banker. **I am always amazed though, consulting clients I am helping get myopic about the interest rate,** losing sight of the importance of doing a deal. Without a deal, no one is going to make money. If a point of interest is the difference in the success of your business, then your business isn't strong enough.

Greg: If someone calls our bank and asks for our rate on a CD, we ask if they're interested in rate or value of the CD. Because it's not just about the rate. Here, we're going to know our customers and their kids' names and their dogs' names. You can pick up the phone and call us. We're not the highest price and we're not the lowest price, but we'll know you.

Ron: Why should I care if you know my dog's name? How does that benefit me?

Greg: Because it's about the relationship. It's personal, it really tells you we care about you, it says you aren't just a number with us. I call it the BALD Rule: Ideally, everyone should have four people that they can call on for advice without fear of being billed. He calls it the BALD Rule: a **B**anker, **A**ccountant, **L**awyer and **D**octor. It's important to cultivate a personal relationship with members from each of these professions — and if you haven't already created one with your banker, this is the time to start.

Terms Used in This Chapter

Champagne phase — this generally occurs during the early stages of an idea, intended transaction or financial relationship. In this phase, everyone clinks their glasses together in a toast and talks about how great things are going to be. The realities that follow are usually less pleasant.

Golden Rule — not the one you learned in Sunday school; this Golden Rule says that "Whoever has the gold makes the rules."

Beauty contest — in business situations, this refers to actions designed to choose a winner. Candidates are expected to look their best from the start.

❖ ❖ ❖ ❖ ❖

Chapter 3

Banking is a Contact Sport

Having the right contacts is crucial in the business realm, and in banking, it's one of the most important assets you can have. From the bankers' standpoint, the more they put themselves out in the community, the more people they're going to meet — and the better their chances are of converting acquaintances into customers.

As a businessperson, it's important to be visible to the banker. So it stands to reason that if the banker is active in the community, a **good way to stay on that banker's radar screen is also to be involved in civic and social activities.** This will pay off in many other ways; it's likely that you will meet potential customers or other professionals who can boost your business.

TIP

Lesson No. 1 – See and Be Seen

Ron: It's not who you know, it's who knows you. In other words, I might not know a certain banker, but if I'm out in the community doing things, the banker might know who I am and would want to get my business.

SECRET

Greg: That's how I met you — you didn't know me, but I knew who you were. From a banker's standpoint, I want to be out in the community, meeting people. Then if you need to borrow money, you're going to think of me, and I will probably know who you are. That's going to help move the banking relationship forward.

Ron: Okay, so once you know who someone is, what kinds of things do you want to know about the customer?

Greg: I want to know that you're confident, that you're experienced in what you do and that your credit report is clean. I want to know that you're a person of your word. It's also a big plus for me if you're active in the community. **I'm a firm believer that your rent to society is your community service.** So, if I see somebody being a troop leader, they are out there paying their rent to society. That factors into my decision.

Ron: That first meeting is really important. I call it a leg sniff because you're sizing each other up. At that point, it's less about how many widgets you're going to produce and how much profit that's going to make, and more about your character and how they feel about you. Bankers all have their own little hot spot and their own little things that help them determine on the leg sniff whether they like you or not. I cannot emphasize enough the importance of preparing for this meeting, and being buttoned up on the presentation. I always tell people they should **send the presentation at least two days before the meeting.** The banker isn't interested in hearing a presentation about a bunch of boring (but necessary) stuff. The meeting will be much more productive if he's had time to review the materials, including a personal financial statement and a printout of **a tri-bureau credit report** (which will speak indirectly to your character, and keeps him from wondering or running a report, adding to your inquiries). **You do monitor your credit report at least quarterly, right, including scores?** But if you aren't buttoned up and ready to discuss the material, you may lose all credibility. Bankers have an uncanny knack to go right to the one aspect of the presentation where you are weakest. You should consider presenting it to a knowledgeable friend, or present it to a bank you don't expect to do business with, and **after you get your teeth in your throat with a strong "No,"** you will be ready for a banker you like and think you are most likely to do business with.

Greg: I always love a customer who knows their stuff, and having the presentation in advance lets me know they are serious, and don't want to waste my time or theirs.

Ron: After they've created that relationship, customers need to **be seen in the bank**. You don't even have to speak to the banker; they just need to see you.

Leg Sniff – The early stages of a business deal when all parties are trying to determine if they will be a good fit. When dogs meet and are trying to decide if they will get along, they sniff each other.

Greg: It's important to keep building that relationship. At our banks, we put the coffee machine in the back on purpose. I want the customer to have to walk all the way through our building and see every employee. And I tell every employee that I don't want the customer to see the part of their hair; they'd better have their heads up and tell that customer "hello." I want every administrative assistant and teller to say "hello" before that customer makes it to the back.

Ron: Customers need to understand that it's all about the relationship.

Greg: It is. The customer needs to feel welcomed. But as a customer, you should want to go into the bank because you want the teller to tell everyone what a good customer or nice person you are. Then, when the doors close at five o'clock, everyone else is going to hear that from them. Those are the kinds of comments that get heard by your banker and they truly do factor into the kind of relationship you're going to have with your bank.

If you come into my bank and you're a jerk to my employees, that's going to get back to me. And it could cost you the business, because why would I want to do business with someone my employees don't like? We have plenty of people who want us to loan them money, so jerks aren't the kind of people we're going to do business with.

Creating Your Personal Financial Statement

Once the leg-sniffing is done, the champagne glasses have been clinked together and everyone seems to be getting along, it's time to get down to business. That means really digging into the numbers, especially the personal financial statement.

TIP

This is where many customers make small but significant mistakes. By overestimating the worth of some of their assets, they can raise a red flag with the banker. **In this area, subtlety and honesty win out over flashiness and boasting** — and it will set the tone for the relationship that follows.

Lesson No. 2 – Don't Overshare

Ron: All bankers have their own little thing that they like or don't like to see on a personal financial statement. I knew one banker whom I took my personal financial statement to, and it didn't list any personal belongings. I was wearing about $10,000 worth of jewelry when we met, but I hadn't put any of that down on my financial statement.

It turns out that a guy who had been to see the banker before me had listed all of his belongings, and he put personal items on there like TVs and clothes and jewelry. Now, we all know that we have TVs and clothes and jewelry at home, but we also know that if we're hit by a bus tomorrow, they aren't worth a thing. But this guy had listed (or placed a value on) all his personal belongings along with his real estate and cars.

Then the banker met with me, and I **didn't list any personal belongings on my financial statement.** His attitude was that the values on the real estate and everything else that I had listed were probably more realistic than those of the guy who tried to squeeze every dollar he had into his personal financial statement.

Greg: A lot of the statements that people give me have the appraised value of their property, so I'll double-check that with the appraisal district numbers. The tax appraisal values better not be too far off from the numbers the customer gave me. If you paid $500,000 for this property a year ago, and now you're telling me it's worth $1 million, that's a red flag for me.

Ron: On my personal financial statement, I **show the real estate and any other large assets at cost AND at market.** This provides the banker with an acid test. If I paid $500,000 for it, and I am saying it's worth $600,000 five years later, he believes it's right. If I say I paid $500,000, and it's worth $700, 000 (accompanied by a story about what a great deal it was), he thinks I am likely a dreamer and/ or full of crap. Bankers are reasonably smart, so don't waste time trying to fool them. You're a lot better off having fewer assets but being really credible than having overinflated assets and not being

SECRET

credible at all. **And he will likely look at the tax district's value of your real estate as well, just for a reasonableness test.**

Greg: I don't want to see that you've put your jewelry or your stamp collection or your arrowhead collection on there. It's much classier to disclose every penny that you owe, but we know you haven't put down everything you own.

TIP

Ron: I always make a statement in my financial statement that the real estate value is conservatively based on my knowledge of market comparables. **This won't work unless you have credibility in this area.** For purposes of the math, it's based on cost. But you have to be honest. It goes with letting them in the tent. It's a lot like doing a deposition: Always just answer the questions you're asked and don't try to add more information.

Greg: And again, that is going to speak to the kind of relationship you'll have with your banker in the future. I want to know that you're going to give me the information I need, when I need it.

When (and When Not) to Call Your Banker

SECRET

After you've met all the customary standards, both personal and professional, the situation should progress and you will have a good working relationship with your banker as you gain credibility with him. Just as with the personal financial statement, it's important to **exercise discretion in how much information you provide your banker.** As in all relationships, it's important to be honest, but that doesn't mean you need to disclose every little fact. Remember, you can't put the toothpaste back in the tube!

Lesson No. 3 – Knowing How Much Information is Too Much

Ron: You have to have a good relationship with your banker, but some people want to call and share every detail, even if it's unlikely to affect the banker at all.

I'm not going to pick up the phone and tell my banker that I just

In the tent also known as Lifting the Kimono – Involved, actively engaged, included in discussions or other activities, knowing the entire plan, not just part of it. Letting folks *in the tent* always lets them know what you are or everything you are doing, but it is often necessary to let them *in the tent* in order to win support. Some employees need to be *in the tent*; others don't because they don't need to know all the information. Often times there is an optimum time to let people in: for instance, after the plan has been worked out and the presentation rehearsed.

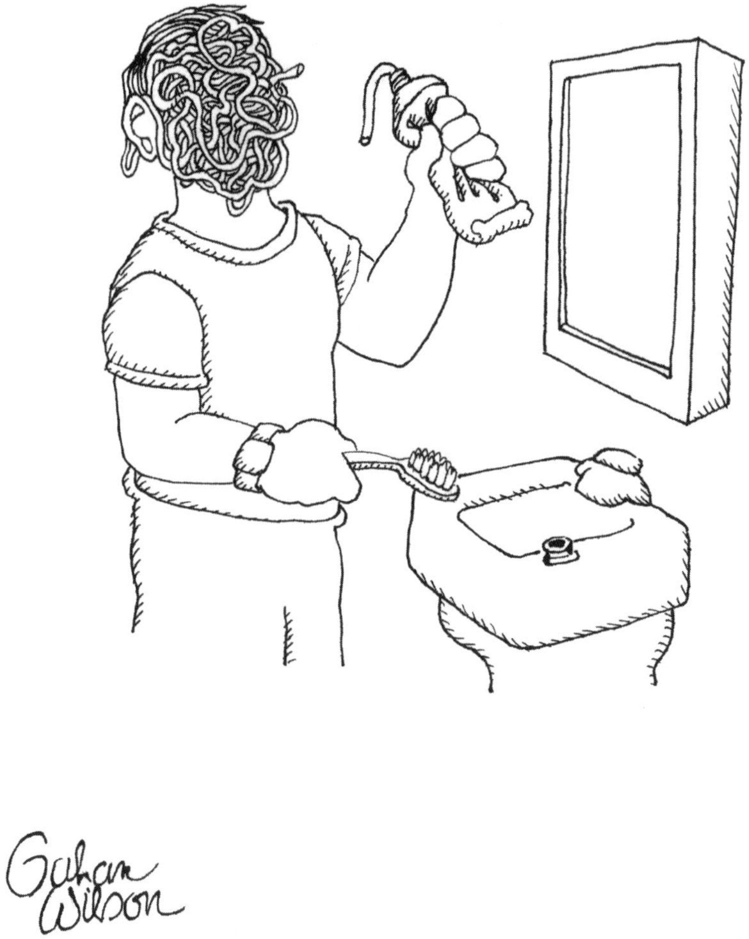

Toothpaste is out of the tube – Something said or done prematurely or without adequate planning, which is now difficult to undo. Like trying to get toothpaste back into a tube, it's pretty much an impossible task.

Use: "Only after we announced the acquisition did we realize the financing wasn't approved; the *toothpaste was out of the tube,* and we were in big trouble."

had a customer fall down in the shop and cut off his finger, when I have insurance. Some bankers will want to hear about that, but when I talk to the banker I want to talk about good things and have positive energy. But I also want to make sure that I disclose anything that's just dreadful or that affects the banker directly.

For example, one of the businesses I used to own rented out exotic cars. A driver rented our green Lamborghini and basically cut the car in half with a tree. When that happened, I didn't call the banker who held the loan on the car, because I had insurance and the customer had insurance. I knew that the insurance was going to pay for the car and it wasn't something that the banker needed to be concerned with. Now, if he'd called and asked me about it, I would've told him about it.

Greg: I once heard somebody say, "I've never killed a messenger as long as they got me the message before it was too late." That's really true with your banker. If you're going to bring me bad news, don't bring it to me when it's too late. I want to know as soon as practical how it will affect you and the bank. And any solutions or actions you are planning. You can ask for my advice. But what I really want are solutions.

The bank wants to know if you're in a lawsuit that's material, but you're right — it doesn't care about something insurance will take care of. However, let's say you have an employee who takes a shotgun and opens fire in your warehouse; you're going to have a lot of lawsuits filed. Your banker needs to know that right away.

If I find it out on the street, it's completely different than finding it out from you. If it's going to affect me, I want to know the good, the bad and the ugly.

That also means that if you're having a problem with cash flow, I want to know ASAP. Don't wait until you're 90 days past due and then call the bank, because by then it's too late to help you.

Ron: The bottom line is, you should share only what's material, and have a solution in mind when you pick up the phone and call your banker, and always anticipate his questions, and know the answers, be buttoned up. A word here about transparency, based on my experience in the serious economic times we have seen recently. I've always heard the same thing. Let the banker know early.

TIP

Sometimes what you know is worse than what you don't know. I never want to deceive anyone. But when I went to the bank to discuss how occupancy had fallen and it was affecting cash flow, it became tense. *Very* tense. *Very* fast. It didn't matter that I had a 30-year relationship. A perfect relationship. The tone changed. I've added this material at the last minute before the book goes to print, as it's SO important.

TRAP

When a bank identifies a loan that *could* be in trouble, it is required to assess how much trouble. They have to note the file and it gets picked up by examiners. There are a lot of complex rules from the regulatory agency governing how such loans should be treated – I won't bore you with them, and the bank has a policy of what to do as well. (This is the part where now what the banker knows is worse than what he didn't know.) Now, don't misunderstand me, the banker needs to know if your cash flow is going to be down and your ability to make payments is in jeopardy. *But* – if you have other sources of cash to make the payments, it may not be necessary to bring it to the banker's attention. You shouldn't hide it either, but always disclose and discuss it in the context of why it's not a problem (you can make the payments anyway, from second or third sources of cash), *and* what you are doing to make it better (i.e., making improvements, bringing on a new contract or new tenants).

SECRET

If in fact the repayment of the loan under current terms is at risk, the lender is required to set aside bank capital, and reserve for the potential loss, whether it be an impairment or total loss. The day this happens you WILL BE persona non grata at the bank. Your loan isn't earning the bank money, and in fact the amount of that reserve hits the earnings for the bank immediately. The banker's first allegiance is to the bank, and the reserve will happen. If the examiners discover that the banker knew of the impairment and didn't disclose it and take an appropriate reserve, the entire bank comes under grave scrutiny. So your relationship is likely a victim.

Recent policies of the regulatory agencies are encouraging lenders to reamortize loans (put them on longer payouts to lower the payment), and to not "call" them if the value of the asset is less than the loan *so long as* the loan is performing. What is "performing"? That means the repayment is not at risk and the bank is stil earning interest. Curiously, however, the regulations still require that the problem loans be identified and capital set aside, so **you are likely done at the bank**. If you happen to have a loan mature while under these circumstances, the lender is likely to not renew the loan and if you can't pay it off, there will be a foreclosure. Not good. What are some of the guidelines that are looked at? (These vary some bank to bank.)

SECRET

- **Non-income producing assets as collateral can't typically be financed for more than five to seven years.**
- **You won't be allowed to pay interest only (a viable way to lower payments) for over two years.**
- **A new appraisal will likely be required.**
- **If the loan is to be modified, there may be fees to the bank.**
- **You may be required to put up additional collateral.**
- **Your personal cash position will be very important. immediately, whereas it may have not been scrutinized so closely before.**
- **Your global cash flows (cash flows from all sources, positive and negative) will be heavily reviewed. You may not have even been submitting a global cash flow statement in the past.**
- **You likely won't be able to move the loan to a new lender, so don't count on that.**

TIP

What advice can I offer?

- **Have the solution before you go to the bank to discuss it. And do so as soon as possible. Don't think the lender is going to just turn his head because of your relationship, though.**

- **Study and prepare cash flows more regularly – and understand them.**
- **Work maturities of loans at least one year in advance if practical. If there is going to be an issue with a renewal, you need to know now, so you can plan for it (in many cases, with your banker's concurrence).**

TIP

- **Talk to business friends about how they hear things are going and potential solutions they might have.**
- **Talk to bankers that you don't have loans with. Find out how they treat such situations so you can plan accordingly. Most banks are about the same, though some that are very troubled may have worse options.**
- **Work harder, faster and smarter at implementing solutions.**

SECRET

I solved my issue. I had three loans with my lender. All three of the commercial properties had very low debt relative to their value, and two were doing well. **The lender put all three together on one extended note, lowering payments.** In this arrangement, the loan to value is good and the debt service isn't in jeopardy. Nothing to report, and no reserves. I was fortunate that my officer was a senior lender, because had I had a "relationship" officer, he would not have had the horsepower to get it done. One other note, I have relationships with primarily community banks and would only recommend you do the same. *Any* of the money center banks would likely have immediately written up the loan as substandard, and the cards would have started falling. But that's just my opinion; I know the money center banks won't agree with this perspective.

Getting the Proverbial Free Lunch

Whoever said there's no such thing as a free lunch apparently didn't have a very good banker. As a customer who has cultivated a healthy relationship with your banker, you should expect to be taken out to lunch by your banker at least twice a year.

This isn't just about getting to eat on your banker's dime; it's a positive way to stay in touch about what is happening with your business and deepening the bond that needs to exist between the banker and his customer. Make sure this happens 90 days before your annual review.

Lesson No. 4 – Making Lunch Count

TIP

Ron: It's really important to **go to lunch with your banker at least twice yearly.** Again, it goes back to that relationship. When we're at lunch, my banker's going to ask me how business is going, then he's going to talk to me about the wife and the kids and the hunting trip and the new boat … that's the contact sport that we're talking about. You need to work at having that kind of relationship with your banker.

That being said, you'd be amazed at how many banks I do business with that don't ask me to go to lunch.

TIP

Greg: If they don't call you, you should call them.

Ron: I do! And I make them feel like crap about it, too. I'll call them up and say, "Hey, what do I have to do to get a lunch? My other two banks have already taken me." And every time they will immediately offer to take me to lunch, and I make them feel like crap about me having to ask them. And they should! I always tease them, saying I should get at least one lunch annually for every million in loans, that puts things in perspective.

Greg: A good banker is going to really work at the relationship. That's why, when I have to go somewhere that's only a few hours away, I'll drive instead of getting on an airplane. That way, I can spend that time "smiling and dialing." I print out my customer base and look at whom I haven't talked to in a while. Then, while I'm driving, I'll call and check in with them.

If your banker isn't talking to you at least semi-annually, he's not doing his job.

Ron: I once didn't establish a relationship with a bank that was courting me because the loan officer wouldn't, couldn't or didn't use email. Everyone has their pet peeves, but I want to communicate regularly using email.

A Good Banker Always Looks After the Customer

As you probably already know, it's not enough just to have a banker; what you need is a banker who has your best interests at heart.

Greg: You want to know that your banker isn't there just to make a profit; they are there to add value to your business. I want my customers to do well. The better my customers do, the more successful my bank is. Everyone wins.

How do you know if a banker is looking out for you? For example, say a customer wants to buy a car and needs a loan. When the customer talks with his banker, he is offered an interest rate of 7 percent. But that night, he sees a commercial and learns that the manufacturer is offering 1 percent financing.

Now he thinks the bank just cheated him. A good banker would tell him up front that he can get one percent financing through Ford Motor Credit. That's what's best for the customer, and what's best for the customer is always right.

The way I look at it, if he's paying 1 percent on the car loan, that means he's saving 6 percent that he can put in my bank. I make more off deposits than I make on the loans, because I'm taking that deposit and loaning them out. The deposits are not my money, they belong to the customer.

A good banker will always do the right thing for the customer because it builds credibility and adds value to the banking relationship.

And when they need money again, they are going to trust me. The customer may not shop me as hard when he is looking for his next loan.

Chapter 4

How Not to Get Your Banker Fired
(And When to Fire Him)

The relationship between a banker and a businessperson is like many others — it requires trust, teamwork and shared goals to be truly successful. As a businessperson, it's important that you do everything possible to keep things running smoothly in the relationship for your banker. **Keep in mind that your banker has a boss, too,** and they both have requirements and responsibilities to meet. Helping him or her meet those duties will go a long way toward strengthening the relationship. Some of the things you can do to make your life easier include:

SECRET

- Understand how the loan approval process works – if you ask, they will tell you. Understand what is required for a loan package and the timing. *Never* be in a hurry, but always have a good sense of urgency.
- Always furnish reports as required, on time.
- If your insurance lapses or you have other items that trigger scrutiny, cure them IMMEDIATELY (as in hours if possible, bankers love it when you have a sense of urgency).
- Always speak to other bank employees, make sure they know who you are and that you are a "good customer."

Lesson No. 1 – Making Your Banker Look Good

Ron: Bankers have to meet certain requirements and it's the customer's responsibility to help them do that. Bankers have a fiduciary responsibility to the bank and they have examiners who come in, look at what they're doing and criticize it, bless it, or

TIP

whatever. So as a businessperson, it's important not to do things that could get the banker in trouble. I'd say the first thing is that the customer has to deliver their financial statements on time. **By the way, think about this requirement when you take out the loan.** Don't set yourself up for a frequency or timing issue with the statements. Bankers understand that it can take some time to close the books, etc., so ask for reporting requirements that you know that you can make easily. Deliver them early. Then they are never on his list of exceptions! And don't kid yourself; they know when your loan payment is late also.

TIP

SECRET

Greg: That's huge. **The No. 1 flag on accounts is when a payment is past due, so don't ever let your payment be late.** A lot of people will make their payment on the day before a late fee is due — don't do that! If your loan payment is due on the first, make your payment on the first, not when you're going to get hit with a late fee. Pay it on day one, every time. I have a report on my desk – as does every loan officer – showing which customers are one or more days past due. The next day it says they are two days past due. Don't think they don't know. **The same report shows them your collected balances the same day.** What do you think the banker thinks when your payment is one day late and your checking account balance is low?

SECRET

Ron: And if you're going to be overdrawn, you should never be overdrawn on the last day of the month. You can be overdrawn every day of the month, which is terrible, but if you are overdrawn (also known as "in the cuts") on the last day of a month, **you are on a report the directors and examiners see.** This also applies to past due loan payments.

Greg: You should never be overdrawn, period. Being overdrawn and being past due are two big red flags.

TIP

Ron: A banker once told me that a lot of customers don't think it's a big deal to be overdrawn, but here's why it is: **All customers who are overdrawn don't go bankrupt, but all customers who go bankrupt were overdrawn.** So the point is, it's a red flag that may precede a failure.

Greg: That's exactly right. And if it happens frequently, a banker is going to think, "If they can't handle their money, why should we let them have some of ours?"

SECRET

Ron: Most banks have internal and external examiners. Internal examiners are hired by the bank, or as contractors, to review the files BEFORE the external examiners come. (External examiners work for one of the federal or state regulatory agencies. When the external auditors arrive, one of the first things they look at is the internal examiners' report.)

Greg: Right. If a bank isn't big enough to have an internal examiner, it usually pays a third party to do that, because nobody wants an [external] examiner to find a problem. I want either my loan officer or myself or a third party that I hire to find any problem.

Ron: So, what else do examiners look at when they come in? They look at the biggest loans, because if those go bad they can take the bank down. So as a business, if you have one of those big loans, you need to make sure you're performing well.

That's one reason that I like being a small fish in a big sea. I like having a $1 million loan with a bank that has a $5 million loan limit. The examiners won't look at a $1 million loan nearly as hard as they'd look at a $5 million loan, in a bank that has a legal loan limit of $5 million. In the world of big banks, where the legal loan limit might be $40 million or more, if you owe $1 million or $5 million, you might not even get looked at. The logic is simple, a loan loss that size won't take the bank down. The exception, of course, is exceptions. If you are in the "cuts," late on a note payment, they will likely review your loans every time regardless of size.

SECRET

Greg: It all does become relative to size. **And the one thing that's even worse than being past due at the end of the month is being past due at the end of the calendar quarter.** Banking examiners look at what is called a call report that has all that information. When the end of the quarter is coming up, I am all over my staff — I don't want any past dues, I don't want any exceptions

— I want everything clean as a whistle. If things aren't in great shape, the exam is going to be a tough one, as they know we had a chance to solve problems but didn't – which sends a message that we are sloppy.

Ron: So let's look at what else examiners look at, like mature loans. (These are loans that have come to their end, unless renewed, and need to be paid off or renewed.) If you have a business loan that's mature and you didn't give the bank the information it needs 60 days in advance to renew the loan, then the bankers are scrambling to get it renewed at the end of the quarter.

And it's not just mature loans that examiners look at — it's all the paperwork relative to the loan, too, like a paper that hasn't been signed or a title that hasn't been transferred.

Greg: They're going to look at large loans, as you mentioned, but they'll also look at every loan on the past due list, whether it's $25,000 or $2.5 million. If you're on the past due list, regardless of size, you're going to get looked at.

Where There's a Rule, There's an Exception

When bank examiners conduct a quarterly review, they are looking for loan policy exceptions — anything that would give them cause to review the paperwork and make sure that the loan is in order. If the loan policy says they require 20% down on all cars, and they make one with a 10% down payment, the officer has to make an exception to loan policy and get it approved.

Missing paperwork is a common exception — it could be a rent roll, proof of insurance or a quarterly financial statement, anything that provides the bank with necessary documentation. But there are other exceptions that customers should be aware of.

Lesson No. 2 – Knowing Your Exceptions

TRAP

Greg: Missing documentation creates one kind of exception, but there's also something that's known as a financial exception.

If you have agreed to keep certain ratios in place, such as a required level cash flow, that's what I consider a financial exception.

TRAP

Ron: What about a loan-to-value ratio when you're making the loan? **Any exception to your underwriting policy goes on a report.** So say a bank's normal policy on cars is that it wants a 10 percent down payment. But because someone is a really good customer, it financed 100 percent of the car. That would be an exception to the bank's loan underwriting policy, so that's going to make its report.

SECRET

Loan to value (LTV) is the amount of the loan compared to the value of the collateral. Generally, **value is defined as the lesser of cost or market,** so real estate must use the purchase price for value if it's less than the appraised value. The LTV ratio can change depending on the type of loan. For instance, cars might be financed at an 80 or 90 percent LTV, unless they have been wrecked and repaired, then the bank might want a 50 percent LTV if it finances the car at all. On speculative undeveloped non-income producing real estate, they might not want to loan over, say, 50 percent of the value. Does an officer have to seek concurrence to allow that exception?

SECRET

SECRET

Greg: It usually has to be approved by either a committee or by whoever inside the bank has the stronger pen, such as the other concurrence officer. A lending officer usually has to go outside his or her authority to get an exception approved.

Ron: So, really, **it's not necessarily a bad thing, so long as the bank knew about it and documented that the exception was waived.** For instance, I have financed wrecked cars. They always document in the file that insurance isn't required until the car is repaired, you can't buy it, and it's not as critical since the car can't be driven. Why does the examiner want to look at exceptions?

SECRET

Greg: It's checks and balances. They want to know if the banker is some loose cannon out there. The bank has to have a reason for allowing exceptions. Exceptions can turn into big problems. Overdrafts, missed payments, documents not in order, insurance expired are but a few that can cause problems. Moreover, the examiners want to see that problems (exceptions) are resolved, it's good housekeeping.

Ron: Do overdrafts make the exception list? An overdraft is a loan and there are a couple of catchy rules connected to it.

For example, let's say the bank's legal loan limit is $1 million, and you owe the bank $990,000. But then today one of your checks arrives at the bank to be paid and it's for $15,000. Let's say you don't have the money in your account, so the bank pays the check – that means it just loaned you $15,000. **And that puts you over its legal loan limit, which is against the law — a bank can't make a loan above its legal loan limit.** If that happens, the banking officer has actually committed a crime.

SECRET

Greg: Absolutely. They can come in and shut your bank down for that.

Ron: So that's the bottom line on overdrafts: The amount your account goes negative is a loan, and in this particular situation, bankers aren't going to do that because they can get in a lot of trouble for it. So, as the customer, you're going to have to bring the money to the bank by its cutoff time that day or the bank is going to bounce your check.

Don't B.S. Your Banker

There are many areas in life where "faking it" can get you through. Banking is not one of those areas! Bankers have access to real-time data, which means they can verify information at the very moment you're giving it to them. Honesty is not only the best policy here; it's the only policy. It's also the only way your banking relationship will have a chance.

Ron: The worst thing you can do is to throw a turd in your banker's punch bowl by trying to B.S. your banker, but then having an unexpected surprise where you tried to fake it.

Turd in the punchbowl – Is another of my personal favorites, slightly akin to *green weenie* but even more repulsive. It's an ugly problem that pops up suddenly and must be taken care of as swiftly as possible. Although unexpected, it usually isn't hidden like a *green weenie*. Also, it can refer to something done intentionally in order to foul you up. (See also: *Binaca blast* for the opposite.)

Use: "At the July sales recap meeting Shawn bragged about his division's results, but CFO Garry threw a *turd into* Shawn's *punch bowl* by noting that the bulk of those results were due to an accrual for the next quarter."

Lesson No. 3 – Keeping it Real

Ron: A lot of people don't realize how much is going on in the background and how much information the banker has access to. Bankers can pull up data on their computers that is current through yesterday's close of business: Year-to-date deposits, overdrafts, fees, cost analysis ... there's very little financial information they can't get access to almost immediately.

Greg: All of that factors in. At some point, every bank wakes up and "stacks" its customers. It evaluates them and rates them in terms of their value to the bank. You want to be at the top of that list.

SECRET

Ron: And it's not just how much money they made off of you; it's also about things like how easy you are to do business with. You might not be the biggest borrower they have, but if you get things done on time and are pleasant to work with, it makes a difference.

But the point to keep in mind is that you should never think you can B.S. a banker, because he or she has all that information: your average balance, your average collected balance, the number of times you've been overdrawn — and that's for the past 12 months, not just the calendar year. So even if you've been clean this calendar year, they still see what you did the entire 12 months before today.

When (and How) to Fire Your Banker

As evidenced by movies, love songs and headlines, not all relationships work out in the long run. The same is true of banking relationships, which may, after time, no longer be mutually beneficial. Knowing when to fire your banker is important.

Lesson No. 4 – Giving Your Banker the Boot

Ron: I've fired bankers four times in my life, but I've never done it to get a better deal.

Greg: That's important to point out. You don't fire a banker just to get a better deal; you fire bankers when they don't give you what you want and have no really good reason for that.

Ron: The first time I had to fire a banker, I'd been with the same bank for a long time and brought my banker a renewal request with documentation. It was information that was needed 90 days before the loan was due. He didn't put it through, so by the time the loan matured, it was headed toward being past due. Then he told me that my timing was bad and that they weren't able to make that kind of loan. I asked him what ratios I needed to improve, so that he could consider it, but he wouldn't give them to me. He told me to go let another banker tell me no and then I'd know the answer was no.

So I went to another bank. It reviewed the credit and within eight days it made the loan and I went back and fired the other banker.

Usually that happens with a wire transfer between banks to pay off the loan, but I asked for a cashier's check because I wanted to do it personally. He had been my loan officer for over 10 years, so it was actually very sad for me.

Greg: A good reason to fire your banker is if he or she doesn't fight for you as a customer. Your loan officer is your salesperson to the bank and if you can't get what you need to run your business, it's reasonable for you to find another bank. Think of it this way — if you go to a doctor and he or she can't make you better, you're going to go to another doctor.

Ron: That's what happened the second time I fired my banker. I was doing some estate planning and wanted to put all my real estate properties into a limited partnership. The title company prepared all the necessary documents and then sent all that paperwork to the bank. I had six or seven banks that it had to go to and some of them charged me small attorneys' fees — less than $1,000 — because they had to have their attorneys make sure it was correct. Others didn't charge me at all.

Then one banker came back and said he'd have to charge me a one-point fee of about $2,500. I told him that none of the other banks had done that and that if he charged me that fee, I would move my loan and the rest of my business at the earliest opportunity. He called back two days later and said that was the best he could do. So I paid the fee, but about four months later, I got a call from a loan officer I knew. He said if I moved my loans to his new bank, which had just opened, he'd waive all my fees. So I did and then I called the president of the first bank and told him I was leaving because my loan officer hadn't fought for me. The bank or the officer had been greedy.

Greg: That's another important point: Always make sure that you have another bank to go to before you fire your bank!

Ron: The third time I fired a banker, it was because he didn't have e-mail. And he was the president of the bank! How can a banker not do e-mail? So I told them I wouldn't do business at a bank where the loan officer didn't use e-mail.

Greg: That speaks to their responsiveness. You want to know that they can communicate in a way that works for you. Bankers should always get back to you the same day — even if it's just to tell you that they don't have an answer for you right now, but they're working on it. I make it a practice to respond to a letter with a letter, a phone call with a phone call and an e-mail with an e-mail.

Ron: Good reasons to fire bankers are because they're not fighting for you or they're not being fair-minded and competitive or they're just unresponsive and not giving you what you need that's appropriate.

The fourth time I fired a banker it was because I wanted to get a fixed rate on my loan, because I thought rates were about to go up. He wanted to keep the rate floating. This went on for months.

Finally, I took it to another banker, who gave me a commitment letter. I called the first banker and asked if he'd sell the loan; he said he wouldn't. So then I told him I was moving it — and within four hours he called and said he could fix the rate. But it was too late. I paid about $30,000 extra to move the loan because I didn't have a banker who was willing to give me what I needed. Another greedy banker, though I've found most aren't greedy at all.

Greg: You do have to pick your battles, but it's also important to know that you can stand up to your banker.

Ron: And there's a right way to fire them. Before you fire them, tell them that they need to understand what your reaction will be to what they're doing. Tell them you're going to shop the loan *before* you do it. If they can't give you what you want after you've told them all that, go ahead and make your move. Of course, be careful what you ask for, you might get it.

❖ ❖ ❖ ❖ ❖

Chapter 5

Money Doesn't Matter
(Until You Don't Have Any)

Every business owner (and banker) knows that money is important. But it becomes even more important when you don't have any. That's where the paradox comes in: The people who don't need money can get it easily, while the ones who need it can't get any. Or so it seems.

Your banker needs to know that you can handle the money you already have. As his customer, your job is to prove that you know how to manage your money and that you'll be a good steward of the money the bank loans you. To do that, you'll have to get your finances in order and make sure that the paperwork is ready for your banker's eagle eye. You simply can't afford to have bad nums. And there's a lot more to doing that than simply filling out loan papers.

Lesson No. 1 – Sprucing Up Your Finances

Ron: You always want to make sure that your financial statements look their best before you go see the banker. That's a huge mistake people make.

One way to do that is by compiling all your financial statements. People don't realize how many different kinds of financial statements there are.

Greg: There are four kinds of corporate financial statements that people need to know about:

- Internal: This is one you keep running indefinitely. It's internally prepared.
- Compilation: This is when your accountant basically puts your internally prepared figures on their letterhead.

Bad num – A bad or inaccurate number, usually in a business plan or other document. The number is either wrong or distrusted in some way.

Use: "Theresa's model included many *bad nums,* so she was told to study her data for errors."

- Review: A review is also prepared by an accountant, but it is much less detailed than an audit. The accountant will make sure general accounting principles are followed and compare year to year for big variances, checking into those and looking for obvious mistakes. A customer might say he wants a review, but I don't think it's worth much more than a compilation.
- Audit: This is where an accounting firm has verified substantially all of your numbers and looked at contracts and other items that are material to your business' ongoing health.

Ron: I think you'd be surprised. I think a review is worth a little more. Let's talk about the way they test a review — it's usually done with variables from a prior period if they have them. So in my case, when they did reviews, they looked at the different expenses as a percentage of revenue, last period versus this period and whether there were any significant changes. If there were, they wanted to understand what those changes were and what caused them. Bankers like them because they are done by a third party, and I can tell you, they almost always found errors we had made.

Greg: It used to be that if you went over $1 million in borrowing, the banker would step in and say compilations weren't acceptable any more. That's when the bank would want a review. Now, it's usually anything over $2 million in lending. But if a customer like Ron hands me a review, that's acceptable. And an audit is even better.

Ron: But an audit also costs you a whole lot more. …

Greg: Yes. So whether you want to get an audit depends on how much credibility it lends you. Your banker may require that audit. When I get audits from customers, it tells me that they have someone looking around, making sure that their own employees aren't stealing from them.

Lesson No. 2 – Updating Your Personal Financial Statement

Ron: Let's talk about the things you want to see on a personal financial statement.

Greg: First off, it needs to have your balance sheet; it should list all of your assets and debts. Then you need to show your contingent liability, which means loans that are guaranteed for others that you *might* have to pay if they don't. Finally, you need to have your cash flow statement, which shows how much you bring in and how much is left over at the end of each period.

Ron: One thing that makes every business owner stronger is having monthly metrics that reflect exactly what is going on in day-to-day operations. Metrics, in addition to financial metrics, allow you to understand the most important aspects of your business, like how many invoices you wrote last month, your labor as a percentage of sales, how many deliveries occurred, how many credits were written, where your customers came from, and on and on. They are critical to benchmarking your results against your own results month to month, as well as offering comparisons to other industry norms. It's one the biggest issues found in consulting: the failure to gather and use metrics.

Greg: As part of running a strong business — and staying on top of the financial operations — it's important to keep an updated personal financial statement. Most people update their résumés on a regular basis, but neglect to do the same for their personal financial statements. Bank customers with significant loans will find that they need to update these statements fairly regularly, but it should be common practice for all business operators. Update your personal financial statement at least annually, but preferably semi-annually.

Ron: One thing that I encourage people to do is to track operating metrics, like their sales every month, and then track their expenses and things like how many widgets they made and how many sales were made per person.

A lot of times, people don't do their monthly balance sheet numbers. To get the full picture, if you do the balance sheet, you understand that the shareholder equity is going up or down every month. Sometimes the other numbers get so big that it's hard to understand, but the equity section of the balance sheet is where everything boils out — the cash flow and all the other stuff. This section will track how much capital you've put in the business, and taken out, as well as earnings. You should prepare a spreadsheet and compare your balance sheet main items month to month to see changes. **This isn't something your banker should or will see or ask for; it's one of your internal documents** that helps you monitor the heartbeat of the business. If your equity is going down every month, you need to understand why, because eventually you will be bankrupt.

SECRET

Greg: And it seems like nobody understands the equity section. That's where your income statement plugs into your balance. It's really important to understand that part of it.

Think of your balance sheet as a snapshot of your company and the income statement is the motion picture. At the end of the month, you want a picture of what the balance sheet looks like.

So now you have this moving picture (income statement) that is going to plug into this snapshot (balance sheet).

Ron: Another way to look at it could be to think of it like understanding the groceries in your pantry and what you consume. The budgets for what you buy and consume are the P & L and what is in the pantry on the first day of the month is the balance sheet. If you eat more than you buy (i.e., don't replace everything you eat) the inventory count (balance sheet) has less in it. . .

What I find crazy is that you can take that equity section from period to period and generally the only thing that changes it is your profit and loss (P&L). So if you take this year's balance sheet and last year's balance sheet, the equity sections should reconcile, meaning you can explain why they changed.

Ron: But I also want to study the changes in the balance sheet other than the equity section — like the cash. Because the way those numbers move, from one balance sheet to the next, gives me a broader picture of the cash flows. The difference in the equity section from one period to the next is important, at a glance; did the equity go up or down? If down, try to understand why. If you can't, get help! **The lender is going to ask, know the answer, and if there is a problem, have the solution!**

Greg: Right. If your receivables went from $1 million to $2 million, that's a huge difference. So why did that occur? That's what you're talking about with metrics — you want to compare cash from one period to the next period.

Ron: Ninety percent of my consulting clients don't get monthly financial statements, and to me, that's just crazy.

Greg: It goes back to my saying, "if you can't measure it, you can't manage it." You have to have those financial statements to run your business properly.

Ron: Some of my clients say that they're too small and I guess there is a point at which you're too small to pay someone to do them for you. But the bottom line for any company is, if you're not getting monthly financial statements, you're in trouble. It's entirely possible and needed, even if your sales are as small as $10,000 monthly.

Greg: And it's not enough just to get the statements; they need to understand them. Having a book on your shelf that you don't understand doesn't do you any good.

Ron: Your accountant can explain it to you, too. I never went to accounting school, but along the way somehow I figured it out. Whatever way works best for them is fine, but they need to understand it.

Here's a good example of how I was able to spruce up the appearances of my finances. Back in 2001, I went to finance my new house. In my whole life I've never had an official underwriting of a residential loan. I've never gone through a mortgage company, so I've never had one — ever.

It's a complicated process, especially if you have a business or a bunch of legal entities and corporations — then they've got to underwrite all of those. So I was worried about being able to get the loan.

I decided that I wanted to go with my stated income, which is no longer possible, but was a common way of getting home loans at that time.

I wanted to spruce up my personal financial statement and the way I did that was that I had sold a piece of property that netted me $1 million in cash. So I took that money and bought a CD with it. Then I got a loan against the CD, because I really needed the money, which gave me a monthly payment and the loan was one point over the CD rate. So I was getting three points on the CD and paying four points on the loan. On a $1 million CD, one point was $10,000 a year.

That gave me a forced savings account. **When I went to get the loan for the house, my financial statement showed that I had $1 million in cash. And nobody bothered to study all the liabilities to see if there was a loan against the CD.** The optics of it were really very easy and it made getting the loan a lot easier.

SECRET

My point is that there are ways that you can make your financial statements look a lot stronger than they might actually be. Especially when people just casually glance at it. And that can really pay off, so it's worth the time and planning to do it. I would never deceive anyone though or hide items. But improving the optics, especially for your "casual" lenders, is always good. Your main bank will always understand it.

Greg: Another thing you want to do as a company is to **retain some of your profit.** The more you retain, the less money you have to borrow.

TIP

Ron: So many people don't do that. I recently looked at a potential tenant who wanted to rent a building that I own. They had something like $10 million in revenue, so it seemed like this would be a solid company.

When the broker sent over the financial statement, I couldn't believe it! Their financials were terrible. They had $1 million in negative equity. They'd made a ton of income the year before — and they had drawn every bit of it out of their bank account.

Greg: That's common. A lot of people don't understand negative equity …

Ron: Which, technically, means you're bankrupt.

Greg: Right. It means that if you sold your company today, you would have to go to the closing with a check. You would essentially have to pay someone to take your company.

Ron: And that's assuming you can even get book value. You might get more than book value, but you might not.

Greg: When you're operating in negative equity, your business is worth less than zero. I had someone not too long ago who ran a company, but wanted to buy his partner out. But they'd pulled all of the money out of the business, so it had a negative net worth of $400,000.

My question to him was, "What are you buying?" He should've told his partner to write him a check just to take it off [the partner's] hands!

When we start looking at negative equity, that's when we find out who the plastic millionaires are. Those are the people who are driving really nice cars, but they don't own anything. All their credit cards are maxed out and they live in nice big houses. That's what we had with this company. These two guys had the houses, the cars — and a company worth less than zero.

A lot of times they think it's okay because if they get sued, there's nothing to sue. And they're right, there's not — but there's also nothing to buy out your partner for either. And if you need a loan or want to lease some space … you simply don't have anything to show.

It's Not How Much You Make, It's How Much You Keep

Making money is good; being able to hold onto it is even better. For many people, that requires a change in thinking. Learning how to look at your business differently is a huge step in transforming the way you do business. Here are Ron and Greg's best lessons for improving business operations, troubleshooting financial pitfalls and retaining more of the money you earn.

Lesson No. 3 – Don't Run From the Tax Man

Ron: Just about everyone has a huge aversion to paying taxes. But that becomes a problem when **people start managing their business based on how to not pay taxes.**

TRAP

What that means is that they don't report all their revenue or they try to minimize their taxes, which almost always means that they have to minimize their revenue and net income. It's actually very shortsighted.

A few years ago, I knew an old man who had $300,000 in cash that he'd taken out of his business over a 20-year period, because he didn't want to pay taxes on that money. Now, if he had just bought some property or somehow invested that money, over a 20-year period, that $300,000 would have literally become millions. But instead, just to keep from paying taxes, all he has is $300,000 in a can.

My credo is that I'd **rather make another million and send $300,000 to the government, because I still have $700,000.** But this is a really common problem I see: Small businesses spend too much time and energy trying to not pay taxes.

TIP

Greg: I've seen that, too. I knew an accountant who told his builders to take everything out of their companies. He said it would help them avoid lawsuits and lower their taxes. So they took the money out and they didn't retain it — and now their businesses have no money at a time when they really need it.

Ron: What happens if those businesses need a loan? The owners take the money out so they don't have to pay taxes on it, but when they need money, maybe to grow a healthy business, they can't get a loan because their company doesn't show any income.

Lesson No. 4 – Build Revenue Before Cutting Expenses

In these times, many companies are looking for ways to cut costs, but that might not be the best place to start making changes.

TIP

Greg: If you don't have money coming in the door, it doesn't matter how much you cut your expenses. The bottom line is you've got to sell something before you have expenses to cut. Too many times, especially now, people think they're cutting expenses, but they aren't.

It's what I call "dumbsizing." They get rid of employees; they get rid of vendors; they're trying whatever they can just to make it through the downturn. But often, it's a better idea to go the other way and try to increase your revenue.

While your competitors aren't advertising, you should. While they're cutting people, start hiring people and you'll be able to give better customer service. I don't always think that cutting expenses is the answer, because you have to do things to keep money coming in.

Ron: That's true, but too often businesses are not living within their means. If their business is off by 20 percent, maybe they do need to lose 20 percent of their employees. A lot of times they don't need as many people as they have, and they wait too long to let them go. I know it's a cliché, but I think that it's about "rightsizing," not downsizing. It's looking at what the company is doing, what it needs to be doing and how you're going to get your company to do that.

TIP

One of the best ways to do that is by **creating a bridge plan.** The best example I can give is of a subsidiary that I had sold to Ford. When we bought it back, it was losing $1 million a month. We had to make changes and we had to make them quick. We had a lot of ideas on increasing revenue and reducing expenses and implemented them, but it took a long time to make all that work out.

We bought the time by creating a bridge plan for the venture capitalists and asset based lenders. We had to show them how we were going to go from losing $1 million a month to making a profit, so we could service the debt.

Now, bankers don't need to understand the details of a bridge plan, but what they do need to understand is how you're going to make things work. Say you're forecasting a 25 percent increase in sales. How will you do that?

Our bridge plan showed, line by line, how we were going to increase revenue. We showed the service type, how long it would take, what milestones we would use, how long it would take to reach each milestone and how much we were going to cut expenses. And we couldn't simply say that we were going to cut our advertising by $20,000 a month; we had to specify which ads would be cut in which places. And we had to say how long that would take to affect the bottom line.

When you make a bridge plan, you want to forecast twice as many changes as you plan to get, because you're not going to get them all. And you have to plan twice as many cuts, too, for the same reason.

It's a huge undertaking, but it's also a very good exercise that forces you to think about how to get your business back on track. So for entrepreneurs who are trying to grow sales or businesses that are struggling in a time like today, it's a good way to be able to look at your business and look at what steps you need to take. A bridge plan can help you figure out how to get back to profitability sooner.

Lesson No. 5 –
If You Have Deep Pockets, You Probably Have Short Arms

Greg: Making money is easier than holding onto it. We all know it and we've all seen examples of how that works in the real world.

TIP

The bottom line is, if you have deep pockets — **which means you have plenty of money — you'd better also have short arms** or you're not going to keep that money for very long.

Deep pockets allow for a rainy day. They let you take advantage of situations that other people might not be able to act on. It really is true that cash is king, and if a businessperson can close on a warehouse in two weeks, he or she can get a good price. But that requires ready cash.

I have a great story about a property that was owned by an old man. The people who had bought up the property around the area wanted to buy it, but the man kept saying no. Finally, he decided to sell. But he told the people who had been trying to buy it from him that he needed $1 million and that he needed it in a month.

The buyers thought that he needed the money so bad and that they could hold out for a better deal. So while they were trying to bring the price down, another person came along and said that they had the money and could close on the deal the next day. So the old man went with them.

Because of that, the people who had wanted the property all along ended up having to pay $2 million to the person to get the property. And that person doubled their money because they had the cash available and could take advantage of the situation when it came along.

People want to know the secret to getting deep pockets and it's really very simple. You don't spend your money and you invest wisely. That's really all you need to do.

Building Wealth

Borrowing money can create a false sense of wealth. True wealth comes only from permanent financial gain.

One of the best things you can do to build wealth is to put your money to work for you. Whether that means putting it in an interest-bearing account, an IRA or buying gold, it's important that you put a portion of your money aside so that it can begin working for you. Keep in mind that you are saving that money for the day when you are no longer working.

TIP

Another great tip for building wealth is fairly simple: **Own your own home.** I know in the current times you have people questioning this, but as a long-term strategy it almost always works out. If you are leasing a home, the only person who is benefiting is your landlord. The same holds true of office space, but with caveats. A young or growing company won't necessarily benefit from owning its own building, but once the growth has leveled off and the company has matured, owning a building is one more way to ensure that the money you earn is being invested back into your future.

Remember, if you are leasing, you are simply helping someone else pay their mortgage. However, if you lease a place for 20 years, the lessee isn't going to hand you the deed to the property.

❖ ❖ ❖ ❖ ❖

Chapter 6

A Loan, Again? Naturally!

Many small-business owners know that they need a loan, but they might not know what type of loan they need. Like businesses, all loans are not created equal, and going after the right loan not only increases the odds that you'll qualify for that loan; it ensures that you'll be able to pay it back.

Loans are a lot like marriages — the right one will meet your needs and keep both parties happy. But a bad one can be costly and will most likely end very badly. So before rushing into one (a loan or a marriage), make sure that you've reviewed your options and understand what your responsibilities are going to be.

Lesson No. 1 – Matching Your Purpose with Your Needs

TIP

Greg: To know what kind of loan your business needs, the first thing you need to look at is the purpose. **When a loan goes bad, it's often because the purpose was bad.**

For example, if a company needs to borrow to meet payroll that means it isn't making enough money. That is a loan with a bad purpose.

TIP

Ron: You also have to look at the maturity of the loan. **If the purpose is a short-term need, it should have a short-term maturity. If it's a long-term need, it should have a long-term maturity.**

Greg: Yes, you really have to marry those two things together.

Ron: People will often tie up their cash, and then they aren't able to use it to grow their business. Maybe they have $100,000 in cash and they decide to take that money and add on to their building.

Now, the building is a long-term asset. It doesn't make money overnight; it makes a little bit each month. So they spend their money on the building and then the next month, they don't have any money to buy more widgets. That means they can't sell more widgets. Now they don't have any working capital to do what they need to do. They have a big building, but they don't have any liquidity.

What they need to do in this case is borrow the money to build on to their building, which is a long-term asset, and because it is a long-term asset, they should finance the addition with a long-term loan, meaning a 10-year loan. Then they can keep the $100,000 to buy short-term assets and handle the cycles of their business.

Greg: Another good example I've seen is where a company goes out and buys a new fleet of trucks. It invests all its money in these trucks and now all of a sudden it can't make payroll. So it has a great fleet, but it can't pay its drivers.

Ron: The owners should have borrowed on terms that reflected the expected life of the asset. **If they plan on replacing the trucks every three years, it should be a three-year loan.** That's a good way to gauge what the term of your loan should be.

TIP

Real Estate Loans: Grounds for Business

Real estate loans prove to be a tricky area for many businesses. While they can be a valuable investment for a company that needs to own its own space, the speculative real estate market has been the downfall of many an entrepreneur.

Greg cautions against real estate loans for the businessperson who is interested in building spaces such as shopping centers or warehouses. While they may seem like a cash cow, the fact is that you'll have to find tenants to make them profitable. Ron has made most of his money over the last 10 years building and renting out such buildings. But he is experienced, and is a great marketer. Make sure you understand all that is required in skills and experience.

Lesson No. 2 - Knowing When to Buy Property and When to Rent

Greg: I'm actually a big proponent of people owning real estate, but they have to expect to put a certain amount of money down and, depending on what it is, they'll have to match the maturity of the loan with their needs, like we talked about earlier.

For a lot of people, their real estate is their retirement plan. Let's say you own a warehouse, like Ron does. He knows that by the time he retires, he can sell it for his nest egg or he can lease it and keep making money off of it. That's how business owners should look at their real estate.

If you're 55 years old and plan to retire when you're 65, you need to plan to have that warehouse paid off in 10 years. If that warehouse loan is on anything longer than a 10-year payout, you're taking money out of your own retirement.

That being said, I always tell people not to get real estate loans if that's not your primary business. If you need it for your business, that's one thing. But if you think you need to build warehouses to lease to increase your wealth, it's too risky. A couple of years ago, everyone thought they needed to own shopping centers. Now you can drive around and see all the empty shopping centers. A lot of people lost a lot of money that way.

Ron: I guess my perspective is a little different. I have people come to me all the time because they have a 401(k) or an IRA or they're going to get their annual bonus check — and they don't know what they should do with that money.

I tell them they should put it down on a rental house. They just need to make sure that the rent they can charge is more than the payment, taxes and insurance. They want to leverage their assets.

TIP

The one asset that people fail to use, and they don't monetize, is their good credit. They don't make a single dollar for having really, really, really good credit. **My thinking is, why not get paid for that?**

SECRET

The way you get paid for having good credit is by financing a rental house. And then maybe you get a second and a third one. As long as you can realistically rent them for more than the monthly loan payment, at the end of a certain amount of years you're going to have millions of dollars worth of rental houses.

Greg: I'm not opposed to that kind of investment. What I'm opposed to is people thinking they're going to build a shopping center or a warehouse and then lease it out to build their wealth.

It's one thing to put a "For Rent" sign in the yard of a house. But as you know, it's another thing to put a "For Rent" sign on a 100,000-square-foot warehouse. So if someone is going to buy property and rent it out, that's fine. But they need to make sure they're buying property at a level where they can absorb the cost if they don't have anyone to rent it.

Ron: I think it's very important that you plan for some vacancy. I tell people that they'll have to think about how they'll make the loan payment if the house isn't rented — you need to have that contingent cash flow. But that's true regardless of what kind of business you're in. And many folks get all anxious about how they might get cheated and the house might get damaged. Yep, it's all going to happen. But the big picture, the long-term goal is to end up with a house that the renters paid for.

SBAs, LOCs and Other Mysteries of Banking

There are many types of loans out there, and for small businesses and start-up companies, it's important to know the value and pitfalls of each. While you'll want to learn more about the specific type of loan you choose, this section is designed to give you an overview of some of the options.

It's important to note that a Small Business Administration, or SBA, loan does not usually fund directly from the SBA. The federal agency provides guarantees on loans that are taken out through lending institutions. Not all banks offer SBA loans.

Lesson No. 3 – To SBA, or Not to SBA?

Greg: Our bank doesn't handle SBA loans and I am vehemently opposed to them. If they aren't done exactly right, if you don't dot your “i’s” and cross your “t’s” just so, the government is going to try to get out of its guarantee.

In an SBA loan, the agency generally guarantees up to 90 percent of the loan and the bank is on the hook for the other 10 percent. Honestly, the only reason people should use the SBA is if they can’t get a loan anywhere else.

The customer has to pay a 3 percent fee to get that SBA loan. From where I’m sitting, I would rather see them take that 3 percent and put it down as collateral for the loan.

One of the problems we see is that with the SBA, you get pretty far down the road in the lending process, and all of a sudden they find something in your past, and now you can’t get the loan.

Let me give you an example. I had a customer who tried getting a 504 [economic development] SBA loan and he couldn’t get it because he had a DWI [driving while intoxicated] on his record. That DWI cost him $70,000 — that’s the interest savings he would have seen with this type of loan.

I guess that there’s probably a place and a purpose for SBA loans, but in my opinion, they are the future commercial subprime loans.

Ron: I think that’s a misconception with a lot of customers. They think that if their loan is substandard, they should get an SBA. That hasn’t been my experience at all. The banks do underwrite the loans, so they only make them if they think they’re going to be good. Don’t try to get an SBA loan unless your plan is viable, even robust. **The banks just won’t make them.**

TIP

I’ve had two regular SBA loans — it was back in the 1980s — and three disaster loans, which were great. They had 3 percent interest and 20-year amortization on current assets. It’s crazy that our government allows loans like that!

I’ve helped at least six or seven clients in the past 36 months get SBA loans, **most of them low-doc loans.** They were people who simply could not have been in business otherwise.

TIP

They’re called low-doc loans because they involve very few documents, the application is two pages, and the agency approves them in three days. It was for something like $150,000.

Greg: Remember that certain banks specialize in certain things. Some banks specialize in SBA loans. So if that's the route you're going to go, you need to find a bank that specializes in that.

Ron: I always tell people to use a preferred lender, because they approve the loans in house and then more or less just ship them over to the SBA.

SECRET

In my opinion, low-doc loans are wonderful for people who are trying to get into business, but don't have enough money or working capital. Everyone I've gotten one for has done really well. But don't forget, the plan still has to be viable. No bank will make the loan just because SBA is guaranteeing it. **Another reason banks like SBA loans is their capital requirements.** Banks are required to set aside or hold a certain amount of capital for each dollar of loans they are make or are exposed on in this case. With SBA loans, they are only required to set aside the capital on the unguaranteed portion. So if capital requirements are 2 percent of the loan, a $100,000 non-SBA loan requires $2,000 in capital, while the same loan with a SBA guarantee of 90 percent only requires $200 in capital. So then the bank can make more loans. And, in theory, make more profit with less risk.

Greg: But it's important to note that the person getting the loan needs to have been in that business before.

Ron: Correct, because the SBA dislikes start-up loans.

Crossing the Line

For some people, a line of credit seems to be the only thing they need to hatch their business plan. But this seemingly perfect plan often can go badly awry. Using a line of credit to finance a business venture is a risky move.

Lesson No. 4 – How to Tell if a Line of Credit is Right For You

Ron: A line of credit, or LOC, is a form of financing that is usually only approved in one-year increments. It's not something I recommend, because in many cases there are better ways to go about getting the money you need.

So many people run to the bank and get 90-day loans (another form of an LOC), thinking they're going to do something like buy a car and fix it up and then sell it. Like most things in life, it takes them longer to get it fixed than they thought it would or it takes longer to sell the car or maybe the parts don't come in when they're supposed to. Most of the time, what happens is that in 90 days, the loan is due and the bank wants the money back.

So then the person who took out the loan has to go see the banker and the banker has to do another loan write-up and get it approved again.

Then if there are more delays, the customer is back again in 90 days, and they have to go through the whole thing again.

Now, bankers don't want to look at loans every 90 days. In fact, I don't even know why any banker would make a 90-day loan, unless he or she thinks it would pressure the customer into doing something quicker to pay it off.

But here's a better way to go about it. Let's say you're going to buy a car, fix it up and sell it. Why not put it on a **monthly loan for two years?** If it takes you a year to fix it up and sell it, then that's fine. Everyone's happy. **A short-term loan creates a credit cliff.** (Yeah, that's right – and the borrower is the one falling off the cliff!)

SECRET

TRAP

I see a lot of people who think they need a LOC, but in reality, that type of credit is suitable primarily for people who have certain trends in their business or have short-term, cyclical uses for cash.

What typically happens with people who get a line of credit is that they get a $100,000 LOC and then they borrow $10,000 on it. Then they borrow another $10,000, and the next thing they know, they owe the entire $100,000 and all they can do is pay on the interest. In that case, the odds are very good that they will never pay it off.

Lenders like to see a LOC rested — meaning that the balance is at zero — 30 days out of the year. So if you do use a LOC, make sure that you have the balance at zero at least 30 days out of the year; if you can do that 60 days out of the year, even better.

SECRET

SECRET

For most people seeking to borrow money to use in their business, a LOC is not the way to go. In that case, **it's better to convert the LOC into an amortizing loan with monthly payments.** In most cases, the lender will do that for you, and it's better for both of you.

One other thing, be careful what you ask for, you might get it. Entrepreneurs typically don't do a good enough job estimating how much a line of credit is needed or how it will be used, so they ask for less than is needed. When they go back to ask for an increase, all hell beaks lose, including a complete review of the business plan and loan. Ask for what you need, and be certain about it. Getting less than you want can actually kill you.

TIP

Borrowing Against Yourself

One of the variables in a line of credit is the **borrowing base**, which is the amount of money a lender will advance against the dollar value of your pledged collateral; it's very similar to LTV (loan to value). In essence, you are borrowing against receivables, other assets that are owed to you or your own inventory.

In most situations, banks will loan a business 75 percent against receivables that are less than 60 or 90 days old, but that may vary. For example, if your company does business with large companies, which often take longer to pay, it's understood that the payment may not occur within 60 days.

This is just one of the variables that are taken into account when determining how much money the bank will make available. Inventory and fixed assets may also be considered, although receivables generally qualify for a higher borrowing base because they are closer to being converted into cash than inventory. So if you have $100,000 in inventory, $200,000 in accounts receivable, and $50,000 in fixed assets, with borrowing bases of 50 percent, 75 percent and 40 percent, respectively, you can borrow up to $220,000 on your LOC. The balance sheet will help reveal the numbers for the borrowing base.

Be careful what you ask for, you just might get it – Almost literally what it says. Be cautious about what you seek or demand because you might get it and it might not turn out the way you expect. I served on the board of an Internet game company that desperately wanted a shot-in-the-arm influx of new subscribers. Unbeknownst to the company, Microsoft named the firm's latest creation the "Game of the Day" and posted the honor prominently on the Microsoft website. In one day, more than 100,000 people tried to download the game, causing the firm's server to shut down, thus disconnecting the firm from the web, which is not a good thing when trying to earn a livelihood online. (See also: *dog chasing and catching the car.*)

Use: "In my early negotiations with Ford Motor Co. I told my friend and negotiator Brian to tell Ford 'to shove it.' He quickly asked me if that was what I really wanted. Brian warned, *'Be careful what you ask for, you might just get it,'* and pointed out that I was risking a lot with my words, as Ford might walk away forever."

Lesson No. 5 – Understanding Your Borrowing Base

Greg: If you have a line of credit, the time factor in your borrowing base needs to match how your customers typically pay, whether it's 60 days, 90 days or whatever.

Ron: If you have a company that owes you money and it's in your 90-day past-due column, the bank obviously is not going to loan you any money for those receivables or the receivables you have from the same company that are in your 30 or 60 day column.

TRAP

Greg: That is called the **taint rule**. That's where, if a company owes you money outside the time frame specified in your borrowing base, the borrower excludes all of that company's receivables. Because the thinking is, if they aren't going to pay you money they have owed you for 90 days, what makes you think they're going to pay you money that they have only owed you for 30 days?

Ron: Simply put, with a borrowing base, the bank agrees to give you a loan that's a line of credit and they're going to advance money on whatever you've agreed upon.

Then at the end of every month you send the bank a report that says, here are my receivables that are at 60 days or less, along with my inventory. And every month, the bank loans you some percentage of those two amounts. So each month you either borrow up or pay down on the line of credit based on your borrowing base certificates and needs.

Greg: More and more, banks are going the way of excluding inventory and fixed assets, and with good reason. Take a sheetrock company as an example. You have a borrowing base with the company; it turns all that sheetrock that it has into a receivable by putting the sheetrock in people's homes and businesses.

But where's the inventory if the business goes bust? It's in buildings and houses all over the city. It doesn't have inventory any more and the bank can't go get that sheetrock.

TIP

Ron: But **building your inventory is a legitimate way of**

increasing your borrowing base. Take the case of car dealers. If you don't give them the money to buy that inventory every month, they're never going to be able to turn it into a receivable. And their business will shrink immediately if they can't cover it under the borrowing base.

Greg: Right. And then that business goes away.

Ron: That isn't good for either the bank or the customer!

Greg: But from a banking perspective, inventory lending can be risky. Say you're financing a roofing company and the builder goes broke. You can't go back and get the shingles off the roof. You're just out. That's why banks shy away from inventory lending.

Lesson No. 6 – Learn Alternative Financing Options

Ron: A lot of banks just don't offer financing for start-ups. Your bank doesn't do that, right, Greg?

Greg: Correct. Start-ups are a place for venture capitalists, family money, things like that. If you're a start-up, chances are good that you'll have to finance your company by your bootstraps.

Ron: In this economic climate, you have to find something you can borrow against for a start-up. You can borrow against your cars, if they're paid for or maybe get a home equity loan. You need to look at what you own that you can borrow against.

Greg: Or you can find someone to guarantee your loan and pay them a fee to do that.

Ron: Are you going to give someone a loan if they come to you with a guarantor?

Greg: That depends. There are two things a banker looks for in a guarantee: willingness and wherewithal. You've got to have both those factors.

First off, if you don't have the money to back up a guarantee, there's no sense in signing it. And secondly, if you've signed it, you're showing some willingness.

SECRET

Ron: I think customers get in the trap of thinking, "I don't understand why you won't make me the loan, because I brought you someone who said he's going to guarantee it." And they think that, if there's a problem, the bank can just sell the stuff that they're financing and get the money back. **They don't understand that the last thing a bank wants to do is find, repossess and sell anything.**

Greg: Absolutely. If you can't sell it, how can the bank?

SECRET

Ron: There's no such thing as non-recourse lending in the bank business for entrepreneurs, really.

Greg: No, there isn't. So if someone comes in and says they aren't going to guarantee their loan or that they're only going to guarantee 25 percent of it, they're telling me that either they don't have confidence in the loan or they have too much arrogance. Either way, it's not going to work.

And here's one other thing to think about: 50 percent of the loans that are made because the person found a guarantor go bad.

Chapter 7

Getting Credit Where it's Due

It's safe to say that everyone understands the importance of credit. In today's business environment, it's virtually impossible to make progress without it. But even though we know how important it is, too few people know how it works.

Credit is complicated and it's based on many things. Gaining a better understanding of how it affects you — and how a banker or lender uses your credit record to make a loan decision — is an important step toward painting a better financial picture for yourself, both personally and professionally.

Lesson No. 1 – Credit: Make It Personal

Greg: People think that their personal credit doesn't affect their commercial credit. But if you don't keep your personal credit clean, as a banker I'm not interested in extending you any commercial credit.

I realize that there are dentists out there whose kids need braces and I know there are even bankers out there with bad credit. But from where I'm sitting, if you don't keep your personal credit clean, there's no reason for me to believe that you'll keep your commercial credit clean either.

So one of the first things that I do is look at someone's individual credit report. If it's not any good, I won't even look at the commercial credit application. It just isn't worth it to me.

Ron: A lot of people don't think about that. They think they'll just start a corporation or maybe use an existing corporation. They probably know that the credit reporting for corporations is very thin, and isn't nearly as reliable as it should be, especially for small businesses.

As a general rule, banks don't make loans that aren't guaranteed. And in this case, the credit is only going to be as good as the owner's credit. So those who think that they'll be able to use business credit or new credit to get a good credit score aren't going to get anywhere.

But that brings up a good question — what does a banker consider to be good credit? What's a good credit score?

Greg: That changes all the time. It used to be that 700 was a great score; now 800 is considered great. Credit scores go from 300 to 850, and the highest score I've ever seen is 820. When I look at a credit report, the first thing I look at is the score. In my case, it isn't the only thing, although as we've talked about, big banks do use credit scoring: If your number falls into the right category, you get the loan. If it doesn't, you don't get the loan.

But that's a big bank. Bankers at smaller or independent banks are more flexible, because we know that there are many things that can lower your credit score.

Let's say you go car shopping over the weekend; they're going to run your credit scores. Every time you run those, it lowers the person's credit score. So, knowing that, I'm not going to base my decision just on a credit score (note that in some cases with repeated requests for the same type of product in a given number of days, the number of hits is consolidated).

Instead, I'm going to look for a lot of the things that drive that score. I'm going to look at things like, do they have any charge-offs, or do they have any foreclosures? If I see a bankruptcy or a charge-off or repossession, that's a deal-killer for me.

What's surprising, though, is that I've seen credit scores in the 700s that had a repossession!

Ron: I think credit scores have become a moving target in recent years. They were stable until about mid-2008 and then, because of the financial meltdown, that all changed. I think the whole landscape has changed.

I don't necessarily agree with you about 800 being the new standard for a great score. Don't get me wrong, I think a score of 800 is wonderful, but I've seen only six of them in my life. I'm sure as a banker you've seen more, but of all of my friends, only one has hit 800 — once.

My wife has been at 800 a lot because she has almost no debt and almost no inquiries into her credit and the debt that she does have is perfect. But I would say setting 800 as the new standard for good credit is setting the bar pretty high.

In my experience, at around 720 you start looking like someone who handles his or her business very well. And at 760 you're looking like you're the real deal.

Scores of 680 and below are definitely questionable, and then the further down the score goes, the worse it gets. Once you get into the 500s, you are way into subprime territory.

One of the things we do in my business is underwrite tenants for our warehouses. Our managers have the authority to move in tenants who have a score higher than 620 — as long as the tenant can handle the standard deposit and the terms of the contract.

If the score is below 620, the deal has to come to me for approval. And if that person's score is in the 500s, we just won't do it — especially if it involves finish-out of the building — at least not without extra security deposits.

Greg: People need to put more thought into their personal credit scores. When I think about personal credit, I think about credit reports. There's so much buzz about credit and I have a lot of people asking me, "What's the deal about credit scores?" They want to know if the scores are a good reflection of your financial intelligence, and the truth is, they're really not! Because your credit score doesn't factor in employment and income; it doesn't know any of that. So your credit score doesn't tell you how smart you are; it's more a reflection of what your character is. Basically, it tells whether you pay your bills on time, or not.

When Credit is in the Cards

Credit cards have become one of the most common forms of credit. They've also become a dangerous trap for many people.

Not knowing how to properly use credit cards — or how much to pay on credit card debt — has created a crisis for many Americans today. And in the current economic environment, many consumers find themselves drowning in credit card debt. Although our society has learned to live on plastic, too many people haven't learned how to make their credit cards work for them instead of against them.

Lesson No. 2 – Learn How to Play Your Cards Right

SECRET

Greg: For a long time, I thought that paying your credit card off every month was paramount to having a great credit score. But it's not — in fact, that actually **lowers your score!**

When you pay your credit card off every month, whoever is looking at your account thinks that you don't have any credit, because your balance is always at zero. From a credit score perspective, that hurts you. But at the same time, I think from a personal financial perspective, paying your cards off every month is good. For many years, I always carried my checkbook with me when I went shopping, even though I was going to use a credit card. And if I found something I wanted, but didn't have enough money for it in my checking account, I didn't charge it, because I was afraid I couldn't pay it off when my monthly credit card bill arrived.

Because credit card interest rates are tremendously high, I still suggest paying them to zero every month. Most of the time, you get this great introductory rate, and then it kicks up to 18 or 21 percent.

But your utilization of credit cards makes up about 30 percent of your score. And credit card companies want to know how much available credit you have on those cards.

Charging everything on your cards isn't good because it keeps the balance high. Your credit bureaus look at the balances on those cards and at the available credit you have remaining. Today, more than ever, the credit card companies want to know that you've got some availability on those credit cards but that you historically don't use but a third of it or so. Because if you've got availability and you lose your job, they know that you can hit those credit cards.

But paying on time is the key. That makes up about 35 percent of your score. Paying one day late isn't good enough. And when you get to where you're paying one or two months late, that's unacceptable. That will really drive your credit score down.

SECRET

Sometimes you might miss a payment or accidentally mail it late, **but you can fix that.** If you have a good payment history, you can call the credit card company. Tell the folks there what happened and they can look up your history and see that you've consistently paid on time. Then ask them to make sure so it doesn't show up as a late payment.

Right now a lot of people are having financial problems, and when their credit card debt gets too high, they file bankruptcy. We've gotten into a mind-set that it will fall off your record after seven years, so it's no big deal.

While that's largely true, it's not the way to do things. The fact is, bad news counts more than good news. The bad news can hurt you, so try to avoid that. The more good news you have on your credit report, the better you look.

Ron: There are legitimate uses for credit cards; you just have to be smart about it. Recently I advised a business owner to use his credit card on a $30,000 deal.

He was trying to get a parking lot built behind his business, and the cost of the parking lot was $30,000. If he had gone to the bank to get that loan, it would have been a complicated real estate loan, with easily $3,000 to $5,000 in closing costs.

TIP

However, he had a credit card with a $35,000 limit that he rarely used, and he also had an 18-month, 3.9 percent interest deal on it. **I told him to use that credit card instead of going to the bank for a loan.** It had never occurred to him to do that.

So that's exactly what he did — he put the $30,000 on the credit card, ended up paying zero closing costs and three weeks later had his parking lot and he's paying it off monthly, with the goal of paying it off before the 18 month period is over.

Greg: One of the mistakes I see people making with credit cards is becoming what I call "point junkies." They get one of these cards so that they can earn miles for a particular airline and they charge everything they can on that card so they can earn more points. They think they're going to get more flying time.

This can be a big trap. There are other cards out there that have cash-back programs that will let you earn a lot more than you'll get in points. So they really need to look at what they're getting from that card. As long as you're using it, you might as well be getting everything out of it that you can.

When Good Credit Goes Bad…

TRAP

The good news for people who have bad credit or weak credit is that you can fix that problem yourself. Although many **companies advertise that they can clean up your score,** the best person to legally and legitimately clean up your credit is the same person who got it there in the first place — you.

Lesson No. 3 – Give Your Credit a Thorough Cleaning

Ron: You can clean up your own credit. I've met a lot of people who want to learn how to fix their credit, and all they have to do is the same thing that these companies will charge you hundreds of dollars to do.

SECRET

Get a copy of your credit report and go through every item. If there are delinquencies, collections and other negative items on there, you need to write each company a protest letter. **In most cases, the creditors will not re-report those items once you've done that and it may help clean up the score.**

If you want a better credit report, you need to protest every negative credit item on the report, even if it's true and about half of them will go away.

SECRET

The best thing is you've saved money because you can do this in about an hour, **and it's exactly what these companies were going to charge you for.**

Greg: That will work with a lot of companies, but I have had customers call me who were mad because they got dinged for being past due on their payments. I've even had people threaten to sue me if I don't take it off their credit report.

But legally, I can't take that off if it's past due. If it's a bank error, I can do that. But there are tons of people — especially when they're trying to qualify for a mortgage or get a low rate on a car loan — that will call and want something off their credit reports.

TIP

And that brings up another point in how they should do this: **Don't ever tell a banker what he or she has to do.** You can call and ask in a nice, hat-in-hand kind of way, but don't say you're going to have an attorney call and make the bank change it. I'm not going to work with a customer who approaches me like that. All I'm going to do is say, "Here's your credit report; your check came in three days late, I'm sorry."

Ron: First, you're right — I have seen problems getting banks to remove information. And you're also absolutely correct that a customer should never tell a banker anything, but should always ask. Don't be combative, because it's not going to get you anywhere.

SECRET

It's also important to point out that a **loan that is one day past due is not generally, if ever, reported to the credit bureau,** so people don't have to be concerned if it's a one-time situation of a payment being a day late. When it gets reported to the credit bureau is when it becomes 30 days past due.

That brings up a really good point about loans. If your loan is due on the first day of the month, it's due on the first, not the 15th. However, a very large number of people pay it on the 15th because that's when the payment slip says you can pay it without a late fee. So they think that's their grace period. Bankers hate that!

What people don't know is that if you don't pay on the first, it goes on the bank's internal report. So when the banker comes in on the morning of the second, he'll see that loan listed. Every loan officer gets that, and they look at those reports every day. They may or may not be concerned about a one-day late payment, depending on the bank, but I know for a fact that they don't like seeing it every month.

When the loan officer sees that on the 16th day – meaning it went 15 days past due because it was due on the first 1st and now it's the 16th – and if the payment amount is large enough, a senior loan officer will ask the loan officer for reasons.

If we're talking about a smaller sum, like a car payment, the banker may know it's there, but he'll expect his officers to act on it. It's not big enough for him to get involved. But if that loan is for a shopping center and the payments are $62,000 a month, on the 16th day, the senior loan officer is going to know about it and he's going to get the loan officer on the phone and find out what's going on.

Greg: I realize that almost all loan documents have that grace period, but people really shouldn't use them. Honestly, the money you save by not paying that bill on the day it's due is so minor. If your note says it's due on the first, it is due on the first! Just pay it on the day it's due.

If it's one or two days past that, nobody's feathers are going to get ruffled. But when it's habitually two weeks past that, banks take notice. We're going to start looking at that.

Some people think they'll pay all their loans on the 15th day and have use of that money until then. But their loan payment might get lost in the mail or there might be some other delay and it ends up coming in on the 16th day. Then they have late charges and that affects their credit — so it really isn't worth it.

On the other hand, if you need credit and you come into a bank and show that you pay your loan on the first day of the month, every time, and you have never been even one day past due — that means a lot more than saying, "Well, I generally pay it on time..."

Ron: Now, there are times when banks will report in error and it can be difficult to get that changed. I've had two situations where they reported in error.

Banks don't just hit a button and run a report on your individual account; they report on all the accounts that are late on a specific day. If someone keys something in and he or she is even one number off — say now it says the bank got the payment on the 16th when it came in on the sixth — that mistake gets tied up in a pool of several thousand delinquencies that are being reported that month. It's all in one big file that goes directly to the credit bureau.

I have had a bank report a delinquent payment when maybe it posted the payment wrong or it got the principal and interest wrong or it posted the payment to someone else's loan or it posted the payment to a different loan that I had with the bank. Sometimes it will post the payment the day after it arrives and that one day makes the difference between it being late or not.

SECRET

Only the lender can get that removed from your record. But here's the worst part: It still won't report that you paid that bill on time. It'll send a letter to the credit bureau saying the payment was "reported in error," but it won't address the issue of whether it was delinquent. I also had a situation where I got charged off to collections for an item beyond my control. When building a new house, I ordered cable to be put in on a certain date. The installer installed it 60 days early, then mailed the bills. But the home under construction had no mailbox, so I didn't get a bill. Then they wrote it off for collections. I found out when the credit watch on my credit report account reported that I had an adverse report posted. I called that day and the collection bureau said they could help me. It was a $120 bill. They could accept payment and show it as paid, but it would still be there as a charge off paid. My credit score dropped 80 points that day. I was so mad! I called AT&T and they said they couldn't help; I should have had a mailbox up. Finally common sense prevailed and after networking with friends I found someone who knew an AT&T executive who agreed (with just one phone call) to write a letter stating it was sent to collections in error. It took my credit score almost nine months to recover, even though this item was removed from the report. **Paying an item in collections or charged off won't remove it from your report.** Make sure if you get a letter from the credit grantor, that its **addressed AND MAILED to the credit reporting agencies,** the collection agency involved and

SECRET

TIP

copied to you. You will likely have to follow up repeatedly to get this correction done.

One other thing that has made a huge impact on credit scores for me is when the lenders report an installment debt as mortgage debt, and vice versa. If you have a mortgage and they report it as installment debt, it looks like you have $1 million in available credit and that can dump your credit score. The lender has reported it as the wrong type of debt – and that's happened to me in several instances.

These are important things for businesspeople to know, because they need to know what they can do to correct these situations.

Bad Credit or Bad Luck?

It's practical to assume that most people will run into some sort of rough spot at some point during their lives. For some, it might be a small hiccup that dents their credit for a few months; for others, it might be a disaster that completely alters their finances.

How you handle these situations tells your banker a lot about what he or she can expect from you in the future. What you've done in the past can make all the difference between getting your loan approved and leaving the bank empty-handed.

Lesson No. 4 – Divorce, Delinquencies and Disease: How to Recover From Financial Fiascos

Ron: Any time you have delinquencies on your credit report, you need to clean them up, or drain the swamp. Your report is going to show delinquencies of 30, 60 and 90 days. Obviously, none of these are good to have on your report, but the ones that go to 60 and 90 days are really bad. Ideally, you don't want to have any of them.

I've had a couple of bankers tell me that the house is the last thing to go. What that means in bankers' terms is that when they look at your credit report and you're late on a car payment, that's bad. If you're late on a credit card payment, that's bad. But when you are 90 days late on your house payment, they know that you're in real

Drain the swamp – A swamp is a messy, nasty thing, and to drain one is a distasteful job. In business, one may have to drain the swamp, uncovering the *cooked books* and *cookie jar accounting*, just to clean it up and get the numbers right. Moreover, it is drained to see what is in it, whether it is fraud or losses or other hidden setbacks, or just bad data and information.

Use: "We had to drain the swamp and work for over a year to find all the issues, including erroneous information and fix them so our credit looked better."

SECRET

trouble because **your house is the last thing you're going to give up.** And if you're 90 days late on that, you are about to let it go.

They know that if you won't make your house payment, you darn sure won't pay your bank, because you'll make your house payment before you send your banker money, every time. So you're not going to get that loan.

Of course, you should never be late on any payments, but there are two things in particular that you should always pay on time. The first would be some $100 charge from a department store, because not paying that just shows irresponsibility. The other thing is your house. Never, ever be late on that.

A lot of people who have delinquencies also have a lot of excuses for them. And you know they may be able to get away with those excuses some of the time, but often they won't.

For example, I was dealing with a potential tenant recently who had some really bad credit in 2003 and 2004. I had studied the entire report and was talking to him about it and asked him what had happened to his credit during that time. He said he had gotten a divorce and his wife ran up the credit cards and really screwed things up, but that he had gotten it all ironed out and now everything was great.

But I had the whole report in front of me and I could see that he had even more late payments in 2007 and 2008. So I just let him keep talking and then I said, "Okay, so what happened in 2007 and 2008?" And the **blood just ran out of his face because he knew that he had been caught.**

TRAP

The point is, he's a habitual late payer. And yes, he probably does have problems, but this isn't about bad luck. I always tell people that I don't believe in luck, because we make our own luck. And if you don't save a little money or put some of it back or learn to manage it a little bit better, you won't be ready when bad things happen to you. When bad things happen, you need to be prepared to handle them.

And the bottom line is that the lender doesn't care about all that. All he or she cares about is whether you habitually pay your bills on time or not.

Greg: That's true, because we hear stories like that a lot. A guy will come in and tell me, "Well, I went through a divorce and my wife ran the cards up." But I'm looking at his report thinking, "Really? Did she run up the Home Depot account? Did she do a lot of shopping at Sears?" Because I don't think she was buying her diamond earrings there. So don't try to tell me that is what ruined your credit.

People use the sob story about getting a divorce and having their credit ruined quite a bit. But banks don't recognize a divorce situation. If a couple signs a note, banks don't care if they go through divorce court and have a judge decide who is going to pay for it.

All we know is that you both signed that note, so you both are liable for it. When there's a divorce, the bank doesn't care who is at fault. All a bank wants is for someone to pay that note.

Ron: Now it's true that a divorce could screw up your credit for a while, so you're not using just the credit score as a determining factor, right? You're looking at the big picture. If someone went through a divorce in 2003 and it screwed up his or her credit, but then you see that from 2005 through today there hasn't been a single delinquency, not a single filing, no negative or adverse reporting — aren't you inclined to continue listening if the credit score is high enough and the use for the loan is legitimate?

Greg: Absolutely. People have hiccups. But I've been divorced and didn't have a single slow pay and we're going to look at what they did before and after that, as well.

Ron: Another thing that shows up frequently on credit reports is medical bills. Now, I don't agree completely that medical bills on your credit report are okay.

They are not okay in the sense that people expect them to be paid. They expect you to pay your co-pay, they expect there to be disputes and sometimes there are situations — I've had them myself — where the insurance company is supposed to pay but it doesn't, so you're fussing and fighting over it and then the next thing you know, you're

90 days past due. Then, if you're not careful, it goes to a collection bureau.

TIP

That's why now I just go ahead and pay the balance. Now, obviously, if you're talking about a $100,000 bill for open-heart surgery and the part that's contested is $26,000 and you don't have the ability to pay, that's entirely different. We're talking about a $65 bill that you're disputing. Just pay it, because you can keep arguing and if the insurer agrees to pay that charge, it will send you back your $65. That's much better than having the bill go into collections. Lenders will look at that $65 charge-off or collection item on your credit report and see it as a weakness in character, because they're going to know that you probably could've come up with $65 if you cared about it at all.

As far as I know, late medical bills count against your credit score. However, if you're in your banker's office looking for a business loan and you have perfect, perfect credit and your score is marginal and the only three delinquencies are $33,000 for a hospital bill and an anesthesiologist for something that happened four or five years ago, I think they will still listen to you. That's entirely different. It's about ability to pay, but it's also about your character.

Greg: It's amazing what people will let go to collections. I've seen charge-offs from Domino's Pizza on people's credit reports. People have this misconception that when a collection item appears on their credit report, they can just pay the bill and the item goes away. It doesn't. That's not how it works.

SECRET

Ron: No, it's not that simple. **Once the debt goes to a collection bureau or the debt is sold, whoever holds it can sell it to someone else who can sell it to somebody else, who can sell it to another company — and on it goes.** Now your power is completely gone, and this is going on your credit report. The collection company bought a note and it isn't interested in your story or your dispute; all it wants is for you to pay up.

So the moral of this story is, never let an item go into collection.

Avoiding Credit Inquiries

One of the problems with getting a loan is that regular inquiries into your credit report can lower your score. The worst damage occurs when there's an inquiry into your report and no new credit is given; the thinking goes that there must be something on the report that presented a good reason for not granting that credit.

One way to work around this problem is to minimize the number of inquiries into your credit report. Most lenders don't like this tactic, but they will honor it.

Lesson No. 5 – Don't Ask, Do Tell

Ron: Greg, you mentioned earlier that every time someone has inquiries into his or her credit report, it lowers his or her score. But it's also true that a certain number of inquiries for the same type of debt within a certain time period — I believe it's 10 days — will be treated as a single inquiry. So it's not going to do a lot of damage if people are out shopping for a car and they get several hits on a report during one weekend.

But anything outside of that period is going to affect the credit score, so you need to get around it. The way to do that is, **before you go to a new bank for a loan, get your credit report. Print it out with all three of your scores and make a copy of it.** Take that to the lenders and tell them that they can pull your credit report, but you don't want them to make an inquiry, unless they decide to make you a loan. **DO NOT SIGN an authorization to check credit, others in the bank won't know about your wishes, and will go ahead and pull it inadvertently.** Bankers understand this process, though its unusual for them. Many will like how you protect your score.

SECRET

TIP

Of course, the first thing they're going to tell you is that they have to run an inquiry. At that point, you can tell them exactly what your score is. Tell them that they can process your application and arrange the financing and once that's approved, they can run your credit. If the score on your credit report is any lower than what you've given them, then they don't have to do the loan.

This also gets around another problem. If you shop your deal to several banks (I never do), each banker that runs your report sees the prior inquiries. **He knows you are shopping the deal, but far worse, he knows that you may be getting turned down and by whom.** That certainly will color his decision to consider your request.

The one thing you don't want is a bunch of inquiries. I have a lot of new banks that call and want to loan me money. If I want to work out a real estate loan with them, I don't let them make an inquiry. I show them my credit report, all 55 pages of it with all three scores and when we get close to closing the loan, they can go ahead and run it — and it has worked every time.

Greg: I think that's a very intelligent way to approach it, because it's one less hit on your credit report. I have people come in for a loan all the time who tell me they have perfect credit and when I run their credit report, I can see that they're lying. But if you can go in and show a lender that this is what the score is going to be, that's a different situation. And I think that's a good way for both sides to be able to approach it.

The Dangers of Co-Signing

People co-sign for loans every day in America. Often it's a parent trying to help out a child or perhaps a relative who wants to see a cousin get back on their feet. And most of the time, it's a bad deal for the co-signer.

Signing your name on that loan means that you have the same liabilities as the person who's taking out the loan — but you're in a more vulnerable position, because you don't necessarily know if those payments are being made.

Ron: My related tip is on **kids' cars, put them in the kid's name and show yourself as the lienholder.** One of my sons left a car in an apartment complex and it got towed. They notified me as lienholder and I was able to redeem it, lord knows what would have happened if left in his hands. Also, I feel better about the liability of him driving around in a car if its title is in his name rather than mine.

Lesson No. 6 – Think Twice Before Signing

Ron: People don't think carefully enough about co-signing loans. They're out there co-signing notes for kids, relatives, friends and employees, thinking that the collateral on the loan is good and, worst-case scenario, if the other person doesn't pay the loan, they'll get the collateral back, so it's okay.

They couldn't be more wrong. I'm here to tell you that co-signing a loan is always a screwed-up deal. When you co-sign a loan, you become the guarantor and different lenders have different ways of reporting the guarantor if that loan goes bad.

I've seen banks that would report the guarantor at 31 days past due, just like they report the debtor. I've seen others that wouldn't report the guarantor until the loan was in default and the lender had to call the guarantor to seek payment. If the guarantor wouldn't pay, he or she was reported.

There are a lot of problems with this type of loan. You've got people who co-sign a $15,000 note for a car for a daughter or an employee and then the daughter runs off with someone or the employee quits and disappears. The next thing you know, the lender's calling you, the guarantor and wanting you to pay.

And that's not the worst of it. If, for some reason, you, the guarantor, didn't get a call and the person you signed the loan for was late with payments four months in a row, your credit was being dinged all four months. I also saw a situation where the guarantor wanted the bank to do the dirty work and repossess the car. But the bank has to report it as repossessed if it does that. Best to be safe and pay off the note since you co-signed it.

Greg: If more people realized that over 50 percent of guaranteed notes get called, I think a lot less people would co-sign these loans. As bankers, we hate doing loans based on a guarantor. There are a few reasons for that.

First, the loans aren't any good unless the guarantor has the wherewithal to step up and pay that debt. Secondly, he or she also has to have the willingness to step up and pay. It takes both of those things to be a decent guarantor.

People come in all the time and say, "I'm going to have my parent guarantee this." Well, that's fine, unless the parent has no cash. Sometimes it turns out that they have an even worse credit report than their kid, but the kid doesn't know it yet.

There's a reason when a bank asks for a guarantee on a loan. Most of the time, it's because it's a messed-up deal — and 75 percent of the time I just won't make the loan. If I call the guaranty I have two mad people versus one mad person.

Keep an Eye on Your Credit

Even if you have the best credit score imaginable, it's still important for you to keep a close eye on your credit. Today's landscape is filled with opportunities for thieves to steal your identity. In a matter of hours, they can wreak havoc on your credit, and it can take months or even years to repair the damage.

Lesson No. 7 – Know What's Going On With Your Accounts

Ron: I've had the police bring me my mail after it was stolen and then dumped in a ditch. And it's not just me; there are about 9 million cases of identity theft every year. Anyone who has some money or who is a high-profile person in the community has an even greater chance of having this happening, which is why it's so important to have a credit watch on your accounts.

I have a fraud alert, which you can get free if you've been victimized by identity theft and have a copy of the police report. With a fraud alert, before any new credit can be issued, the company making the loan has to call you at the number you gave to the bureaus and verify that it's a legitimate request. You can get a 90-day fraud alert without a police report, but if you've been a victim of identity theft and have a police report, the alert lasts up to seven years. **MAKE SURE you get a police report** on an attempted or actual identity theft. It can really save your butt later.

TIP

I also **get a credit watch,** which costs about $10 a month. It provides you with instant notification if anyone pulls your credit score. You're going to know immediately if someone is trying to get credit in your name.

TIP

It also lets you know what's being reported about you and you can get your score every month and look at what's on there.

A lot of people haven't looked at their credit scores in years and they might be surprised to find out what's on there! In my case, I hate to pay bills. And before technology gave us so many options, the way I paid my bills ended up hurting my credit. Back in 1976, I went to buy furniture and got turned down. It was only $2,000 and I couldn't believe that I'd been turned down! So I looked at my credit report and there were something like 10 or 12 small delinquencies on there that added up to about $200.

What had happened was that I just hated paying bills and it made me sick because I'd had the money to pay them. So what I ended up doing was taking all my bills to my bookkeeper and delegating that task to him.

Even if you don't have a bookkeeper, there are ways you can make sure this doesn't happen. You can set up your bank account to give you automatic alerts or you can just mark it on your calendar. That way, if a bill doesn't show up, you'll pay it anyway and won't get hit with any late charges or get your credit dinged. The bottom line is that you should always make at least the minimum payment, and be sure to make it on time.

Kicking the Buckets

Types of loans are divided into three buckets, and while their criteria and dollar amounts may differ, credit scores will affect all three in exactly the same way:

1. Business loans and miscellaneous larger loans: This is for companies that might need a $100,000 line of credit or for someone who is taking out a much larger car loan, such as for a Lamborghini. It could also apply to a debt consolidation loan, although you never want to ask for a debt consolidation loan if you can avoid it. That type of loan gives the appearance that you didn't handle your business well and could affect you in future dealings.

SECRET

A relationship officer doesn't handle these loans; typically, an administrative person will take the application and, while he or she might have a hand in approving it, it generally is going to be moved up the ladder to a small-business lender. These lenders will have a little more experience than a junior administrative person and they'll look at the credit score. It's not so much that they're going to use that score to decide if the loan is right; rather, they want to see if anything's wrong with your credit.

If the score is fine, they'll look at the proposed use of the loan, the collateral being offered, the customer's character and the customer's experience. Every lender has certain criteria that it uses. The criteria can't be completely subjective, because there are regulations that prohibit discrimination based on race or gender. But each lender has its own underwriting criteria for that type of loan and those scores will help determine whether the customer qualifies.

2. Cars and small consumer loans: This area includes items like department store credit cards and small home purchases, such as a washer/dryer or personal electronics, that are made at stores like Sears and Best Buy. Most of these loans are quick transactions that are handled in the store. They'll be authorized by someone who has a title such as "relationship officer," which is basically **a bogus term for a junior administrative** person who does nothing more than take down your personal information and run it through the computer. That system gives that person your credit score, your available collateral and your employment information. It's very cut-and-dried: If the score qualifies you for a loan, you'll receive it.

SECRET

3. Real estate loans: A real estate loan is almost always going to go to a more sophisticated lender than other types of loans. The person handling the loan will probably have done real estate loans before, and different banks have different policies about how they approach them.

On a real estate loan, whether it's business or personal, they will run what's called a Tri-Bureau Report. There are three credit bureaus out there and all three of them use different secret scoring mechanisms. **Some mortgage companies will average the three scores together; some take just the middle one and some might drop the bottom and average the top two scores.** It varies from one company to the next, although most companies average the scores.

SECRET

Placing Fraud Alerts and Credit Freezes

To place a fraud alert, call one of the three credit bureaus or go to their Web sites:

- Equifax: 800-525-6285, www.equifax.com
- Experian: 888-397-3742, www.experian.com
- TransUnion: 800-680-7289, www.transunion.com

Some of the credit bureaus now allow and or require corrections or disputes to be filed on line.

To put a freeze on your report, send certified letters with proof of identity and address with any required fees.

- Equifax Security Freeze, P.O. Box 105788, Atlanta, GA 30348
- TransUnion Fraud Victim Assistance Dept., P.O. Box 6790, Fullerton, CA 92834
- Experian Security Freeze, P.O. Box 9554, Allen, TX 75013

❖ ❖ ❖ ❖ ❖

Chapter 8

Tips & Traps

If you've made it this far, you realize that there's a lot of information that entrepreneurs need to acquire before approaching their banker. The prior text had trips and traps noted, but some require more explanation, so we've added them here in this chapter. These are necessarily more or less important, just presented with more information. But even with all the information you've been given, there are a few more things you should be aware of before you walk into the bank.

There are certain things your banker isn't going to tell you. But that's why you're reading this book! Learning these tips and traps can save you time, money and headaches down the road. Most of the information in this chapter comes from Ron, from an entrepreneur's perspective, though Greg has certainly got plenty of lessons to teach about getting everything to look its best and get good results for all parties. Most of the material is from Ron, he's an out of the box experienced thinker, and has learned many of these the hard or expensive way. But as with tip No. 19, he hired a good tax lawyer to help with the single member LLC to save costs. Remember, you don't know what you dont know, and it's important to surround yourself with people that know more!

Tip No. 1 – Appraisals Aren't Always Needed

Although appraisals are very common on real estate deals, **you may not need one if the property's value is below a certain dollar amount.** The threshold varies by bank.

SECRET

Banks can use tax district appraisals, depending on the loan-to-value ratio, rather than conducting a new appraisal. In the current economic environment, the Fed is concerned that local tax districts can't keep pace with rapidly changing property values, because tax districts look at property on only an annual basis. But if the district says a piece of property is worth $200,000, a customer could likely expect to borrow $100,000 on that property — or 50 percent of the estimated value — without a formal appraisal.

Tip No. 2 – All Appraisals Are *Not* Created Equal

In commercial real estate, there are two kinds of appraisals: Full scope and limited scope. In a full-scope appraisal, the property is inspected thoroughly, while a limited scope requires less information. Typically, a limited-scope appraisal is all you'll need.

Three factors are considered when a property is appraised:

- Cost: What's the cost to rebuild this building?
- Income: How much revenue can you generate by renting this space?
- Comparable sales: What would be the price if you wanted to sell this property?

Keep in mind that customers can't choose their appraisers. Regulations require bankers hire the appraiser. In the interest of fairness, you can ask your bank to put the appraisal out to bid. The rules have changed dramatically in recent years, so you can't put it out to bid yourself. The new federal guidelines require the lender to get the appraisal and because of the more cautious approach, the odds are very good that the appraised value will be much less than you expected.

SECRET

There are times that a **lender can ask for an updated appraisal** with a limited scope or a "drive by" update or "desktop," and any of these can save the customer money. Don't be afraid to ask. Factors such as performance of the loan and or customer, amount of loan and how old the existing appraisal is can guide these decisions by your officer.

Tip No. 3 – To the Points

Points — the additional, up-front fees paid instead of higher interest rates — used to be fairly negotiable in real estate loans. With money less readily available in today's economic climate, that has changed. Today, 1 point is standard as an origination fee on a real estate loan.

A point is pure income for the bank. There are no costs associated with it, and if the bank wants, it can reduce the fee to half a point or zero. In most cases, it doesn't. But you won't know unless you ask, because chances are the bank isn't going to offer.

SECRET

The negotiation of points depends largely upon your repayment ability. If you're going into the deal without any money, you're going to have to pay a 1 percent fee or even more. But if you have a great deal of money, the odds of getting the fee down to half a point (or zero) are much better.

Lenders can also charge fees on commercial lines of credit. They can charge a point on that line of credit or they might even charge an "unused fee." An unused fee is similar to having a line of credit; it means you want to have money available to you as a loan, but since you aren't using the money, the banker can charge a fee on it. Many lenders don't charge a fee, but expect to pay a commitment fee or unused fee that could be 1 to 3 percent of the loan or the unused amount. The reasoning is that they have to "save" deposits and capital to offset your line of credit in case you decide to use the money, so they want to earn something for keeping that money available, and because they have processing costs related to putting your credit in place, even if you don't use it.

Tip No. 4 – Utilize Note Payable Shareholder Equity and Taxes

For a small-business owner whose company needs capital, the common response is often to get a loan. However, for those who are in a position to do so, there are certain advantages to putting personal capital into the company in the form of a loan.

The capital can be loaned as a note payable to the shareholder. You already paid taxes on the money when you earned it and putting it into your company as capital would mean that it would be taxed a second time if you took the money out as a distribution. If you make the money available as a loan, it's a good idea to charge interest, although the IRS does have strict guidelines on that. However, if you make it a loan, the bank may require you to subordinate it, which means you agree not to pay yourself back until you have paid the bank back or it gives you permission. This means your money wouldn't be accessible if you needed it.

When the money is given as a loan, those dollars won't be taxed when they're repaid to you unless the IRS decides the payout is a dividend and not a loan payment. (This is where a good accountant can help you navigate through potential traps.)

Here's an example of why this makes good business sense. Let's say that you, the businessperson, have $100,000 in a personal savings account. Meanwhile, you own a company that owes the bank $100,000.

Rather than let the money earn marginal interest in the bank, a better use of that money would be to loan it to your company. Charge your company the same interest rate that the bank would charge, whether it's 7 or 9 or even 10 percent.

Suddenly, that money from your savings account is working harder for you. It's making money, because you're earning the interest that would have gone to the bank. Just by looking at the bottom line it's obvious that this is a much better use of the money; invest it in your own company and make some money off of it!

Not everyone wants to do this. In some cases, individuals might want the liquidity of the $100,000 that they have in savings. And the banks will perceive the money as liquidity.

SECRET

Ron: Most lenders will view shareholder debt as capital, if you aren't paying yourself back. **To make the optics of the balance sheet look better,** show it under long-term liabilities as the last item or create a separate long-term liability section and put it last - just before the owner equity section. The lender or examiner may treat it as capital, which improves the fundamentals of your statement.

Tip No. 5 – Use Cost Allocation to Your Benefit on Real Estate Construction and Even Real Estate Purchases

SECRET

Ron reports that he has used **cost allocation** to minimize his income taxes fairly dramatically. It's important to understand how to use cost allocation on new construction or even on a current building being purchased, if possible. To do this effectively, you need to find an accounting firm or a specialist that can do it well.

Ron: I took a course and learned the fundamentals, but since I oversee construction myself that made it much easier to understand and execute.

When you construct a building, the IRS allows you, as the owner, to take depreciation on most of it for 30 years. Some of the other assets — such as the parking lot, the fences, and the like — can be depreciated for 10 years.

Deeper in the code, you'll find the depreciation allowances on such things as site lighting (five years). Certain types of doors, walls and fixtures are listed as five-year or seven-year assets.

For a business owner, it's extremely valuable to have an accountant who understands cost allocations and can help leverage them. This allows you to get more depreciation early, which means you reduce your reportable income without affecting your cash flow.

This is a non-cash expense, so it's a very good way to save money by reducing your taxes in the early years. Another thing to consider is that real estate is unlike any other asset. Every other asset you need for your business is going to depreciate. And in most cases, such as computers and company cars, that depreciation is very real. Those assets are going to wear out and eventually they'll need to be replaced.

Real estate is the one area where depreciation is less real, especially on newer property. Even though your building may depreciate, in most cases, inflation or the increased value of the property will offset the depreciation.

Tip No. 6 – Know Your Real Estate Loan Defaults

Ron believes that this is one thing that every entrepreneur needs to know about! In recent years, attorneys have come up with new paperwork that lists "death" as an instance of default in real estate loans. So if you get squashed like a bug on the way home from work, its possible your spouse would immediately get a letter saying that the loan has been called and that the bank requires the payoff right away.

As outrageous as this sounds, the idea has its origins in sound stewardship; it evolved from business loans where there was a concern that, if the owner died, there would be no one around to run the business. Obviously, things aren't likely to go well in that situation. So the bank wanted to make sure that in those instances, it could get its money back. Businesses assets can go away very quickly following an owner's death. Real estate is much less likely to change following a death. Ron won't allow the provision and **most lenders will remove it if asked, depending on your total situation. You can mitigate it with life insurance as well. He also negotiated with one lender to have a provision that said that the bank *could* cite his death as an instance of default ONLY after 180 days following his death.** Note the emphasis on "could:" Banks don't want good loans to go away, so if the spouse can keep the boat floating, it's likely to be okay.

SECRET

But that's not always the case, and you need to make sure that this default cause isn't included in any of your loan papers. Before you sign any documents, look at them carefully and review what constitutes an event of default. If your death is listed as a cause of default, have the bank take it out! The larger the bank, the harder it might be to get the clause stricken from the terms, but you owe it to your family to make sure it's removed.

While we're on the subject of dying, this is a good time to throw in a bonus tip: Never run a business without life insurance! It's not fair to saddle your heirs with your mistakes. Life insurance is a great way to insure your wealth — and to make sure that your family will be provided for if something happens to you. (Wouldn't you rather have them be able to pay off the loans to the business and sell it than to have the bank take it away from them?)

TRAP

Last of all, when you're buying life insurance ***always*** **buy term insurance** and never buy whole life. Insurance salespeople make more commission on whole life, so they often push it hard, but term is always the way to go. There may be circumstances where term insurance isn't a good fit, but get that advice from someone other than the person selling you the insurance.

Tip No. 7 – Always Review Your Rent Rolls!

Whether you own commercial or residential property, you're going to have to show the bank your rent rolls. A rent roll is a list of tenants that generally includes the lease amount, the square footage and the lease expiration date for each property or tenant.

Your loan agreement will determine how often you must give the bank this information. It works to your advantage to arrange to provide that annually, although some banks want to see the rent rolls quarterly, particularly if the loan is greater than $1 million.

In the current economic climate, regulators are asking banks to provide this information regularly; they want to know the number of tenants a customer has, as well as the occupancy and vacancy rate. They're also **keeping an eye on the maturity of the leases,** so it benefits you, the owner, to have tenants with leases of two years or more and it's advisable to stay ahead of lease renewals.

TRAP

So what can you do when you have a tenant who doesn't want a lengthy lease? There are legal ways around this that can benefit both you and the tenant. One of the best practices is to offer a four-year lease, but **allow the tenant to get out of the lease after two years by providing adequate notice, such as 90 days before the 24th month of the lease.** (You don't want to hide this from your banker, but you don't necessarily need to advertise this arrangement, either.)

SECRET

This allows you to show a four-year lease on your rent rolls, which looks better to the bank and to the bank's regulators. And they aren't the only ones who'll want to see rent rolls — the company that insures your property will want to see them as well and insurers also see tenants with longer leases as better risks.

While we're on the subject, this is a good time to point out that insurers and lenders are often very interested in the types of business your tenants are in. They aren't going to want something that's a liability risk, such as a tattoo shop. Again, you need to be honest, but a little creativity might not hurt. For example, say you have a tenant that's an automotive body shop. Auto body shops are known to be a high fire risk, so you might want to list that tenant simply as "auto repair," which doesn't have quite the same stigma attached. Or, if your tenant sells skateboards or gaming supplies, you might want to simply list it as a "retail" shop.

Tip No. 8 – Keep Your Loan Amount Private – Save Taxes!

Whenever you finance a piece of property, the deed of trust becomes part of the public record. The dollar amount of your loan is listed on that deed.

The official reason is that, in the event of foreclosure, the lenders and courts want to be able to identify each loan very specifically. However, the reality is that the dollar amount isn't going to be the only way to identify that loan. (Let's face it: The chances are good that you didn't take out additional loans on other pieces of property on that exact same day for the same amount of money. So the records showing a loan being taken out on that piece of property should be sufficient to connect the deed to the property.)

When the dollar amount of a loan is included on a deed, the taxing district can use that information to make assumptions as to the sale price. Most likely, the district will assume that the loan amount represents a certain percentage of the value of the property, so it will automatically assess it under that assumption, which could lead to a higher value and tax rate.

Let's say you have a piece of property you bought 20 years ago; now it's worth $5 million. You don't have a loan on it and the tax district's assessment puts the value of the property at $800,000. If you go to the bank and borrow $4 million on that piece of property and the tax district sees that amount, it's going to raise the estimated value of the property. Generally, the tax district assumes that the loan is equal to 80 percent of the property's value, so it computes a value based on that formula and raises your taxes accordingly. With that value in place, the district will challenge you to produce the sale documents to protest, so you lose. In some states, disclosure of sale prices is mandatory; rules vary. So **it's to your benefit as the property owner to keep that amount private.** Legally, if someone from the taxing district called the bank and asked for the amount of the loan, the banker would be barred from telling them. That same sort of confidentiality should be allowed on paperwork that is being filed with the tax district. In Ron's stomping grounds of Fort Worth, Texas, the tax rate runs about 3 percent of value, so the increase described above triggers additional property taxes of $120,000. Yep, over $2,000 per week JUST for taxes. Most lenders on commercial loans will be willing to leave the amount out; however, it's much trickier on residential loans.

Just as with other business transactions, you **can use a non-disclosure agreement, or NDA, to keep the details private.** This can also be placed as a requirement in the contract on a real estate sale, ensuring that you are able to keep the information private. One added benefit is also that you don't want everyone knowing what you paid or sold a property for.

Tip No. 9 – Keep Your Sales Price Private, Too!

For many reasons, it's also important to keep the sales amount of real estate transactions private, too. One way to do this is to put a non-disclosure agreement in the purchase contract. The non-disclosure agreement prohibits the buyer and the seller from revealing the dollar amount of the transaction.

Some states require you to include that information, so check your state laws before pursuing this agreement. You can always **add**

a non-disclosure clause; just include a provision excepting those professionals or employees involved in the transaction who need to know (like the party's accountants) or as required by law.

Tip No. 10 – Don't Stew Over a Boilerplate

Who doesn't hate boilerplate in legal documents? Just trying to read through all the fine print seems to take days. It's an eye test!

Here's the bottom line on boilerplate: It isn't negotiable. It doesn't matter if you find something in there that you really don't like or aren't comfortable with; you won't be able to negotiate it out of the contract. So don't waste your time. And if you really read it all, you won't want to do the loan. But don't confuse this with being careless or dismissive about terms of the debt. This tip is especially in standard residential loans, especially those insured by FHA and other type lenders.

Tip No. 11 – Give the Bank What It Wants: Your Money

Do you know why a bank gives you a loan? No, it's not because it thinks you're a great person and it isn't because the banker is so nice that he or she just wants you to be happy.

Banks give you loans because they want your deposits. They want to have the rest of your money, so they are willing to give you some money to entice you to bank with them. Typically, the credit committee that approves the loans is going to want to do business only with people who give that bank their deposits.

So, what if you already have a primary bank that handles your main accounts, but you want to get a loan from another bank?

The answer is simple: The best way to get the loan — without moving your existing primary account — is to buy a **CD from the target bank and then take out a loan against the CD.** And don't forget that this can enhance your financial statement optics. If you are going to need the interest from the CD to make your payment on the loan, **make sure it's deposited into a separate account** and not added back to the CD, which is typical.

Eye test – A chart or other presentation where the text is so small that no one can read it. The term is often used to describe presentation slides (such as Power Point) with too much data. Presentations should be an overview, not a long list of details. It also is used when referring to the tiny print in any contract, the *boilerplate*. (See also: *mice type*.)

Use: "It was a real *eye test*, with slide after slide being crammed with text."

Tip No. 12 – Negotiate Your Loans

In a real estate loan, the bank will typically give you terms; for example, let's say it gives you a 15-year term with five-year call provisions (or maturity). What that means is that you make the payment based on a 15-year loan, but the call provision means that the balance of the loan is actually due at the end of the first five-year period.

These kinds of loans aren't working out very well in the economic downturn for borrowers. Because of call provisions, property owners are finding that their loans are now due and they can't get anyone to finance it, so the property may go into foreclosure.

Here's a good way to avoid that situation. At the beginning of the negotiation process or in the fourth year of the loan, start negotiating to convert the call provision into another five-year interest agreement. The interest rate might be keyed to the prime rate; it might be 2 points over prime, but at the end of five years, instead of becoming due, it automatically renews for five more years at that rate.

Talk with your banker about converting calls into interest rate adjustments because, particularly in today's market, it's your best bet for holding onto your investment. What if your situation has weakened? **It's much better, and most lenders will agree to rate adjustments at some point in the term of the loan rather than a call.** It actually can benefit them as they have less exposure to rate fluctuations.

SECRET

Tip No. 13 – Get an Environmental Report Before You Sell

An environmental report is required before most commercial real estate loans can take place. If you're selling a piece of property, or just refinancing it, federal law may require you to get an environmental report called a Phase One. (In some cases, a Phase Two, which is more comprehensive, might be required.)

TRAP

Once a report has been issued, any problems noted in it have

TRAP

to go through strict EPA remediation procedures before the loan can proceed, if it can proceed at all. That means lots of red tape and, you guessed it, additional expenses. Big expenses.

A better plan of action is to, independently, contact an environmental expert. You can find companies that do this type of work either online or in the phone book, or you can ask your friends to recommend companies they've used before. Whatever you do, don't ask the bank, because you want an assessment that's independent of the transaction. **Once you've found that company, hire it to come out, walk the land with you, and point out what needs to be fixed.** You might be surprised at how a very small thing can add up to a very large sum of money quite quickly; it might even keep you from getting a loan.

Here's an example of just how important this is: A few years ago, Ron was getting ready to sell a piece of property that had, for many years, been an automotive junkyard. Unaware that he should have had an environmental expert review the property with him first, he allowed a firm to come out and do a phase one inspection for the buyer.

The inspector noticed a quart-size oil can on a small mound of dirt. The can had been turned upside down, and so the EPA decided it needed to check the dirt for contamination. Ultimately, it required Ron to have the dirt hauled to a landfill designed specifically for environmentally sensitive materials. That single oil can on the mound of dirt ended up costing Ron $10,000.

After you have the inspector walk and show you potential issues, SOLVE THEM, assuming they aren't material. DO NOT ask for a written report. **Now call a *different* inspector to do the phase one, or allow the bank to order it.** You will be asked to furnish all reports concerning environmental matters and you can't lie about material items, but you will be much more likely to get a clean report.

What is a clean report? The banker will most likely look at the executive summary, usually one page. It will either say no issues were found and no further action is recommended, OR it will list issues. **If that first page is clean, you are likely home free.** The rest of the report is a LOT of technical gobbledygook. Ron is as environmentally sensitive as anyone and insists you simply should never lie about serious environmental matters, but you can improve your odds of not having trouble with some preemptive work.

Tip No. 14 – Ask the Lender to Sell Your Loan Instead of Paying it Off

SECRET

Instead of paying off a loan, ask the lender if it will sell the loan, which will minimize your costs if you are moving it or refinancing it with another lender. There are costs associated with every new loan: You have to get an environmental report, and a survey and you have to pay origination fees. You might also need to get another appraisal.

However, if the original lender sells the loan to a new lender, all of the protections afforded by underwriting automatically transfer with the loan. (Of course, the new lender is going to want to see all the documents before buying the loan.) The new lender is also protected from any additional liens that might have occurred since the first loan was made.

As a general rule, lenders don't like to sell loans, because they don't want to make it easy on clients to move the loans and as good businesspersons they want the maximum amount of interest they can earn. They want the income from that loan, so they make it hard for clients to move their business to a new lender. They're not being mean; it just makes more sense for them, financially, to hold onto the loan.

In the most amicable of arrangements, or with a fee, many lenders will be willing to sell the loan to a new lender. This can be much less expensive for both the borrower and the new lender, even if the original lender charges a fee such as one month's interest. If the original lender is going to lose the loan, it's more palatable to at least get one month's unearned interest as an incentive to sell it.

Tip No. 15 – Get New Money on Existing Loans

On real estate loan, you can't get new money after the loan is fully funded in most states. Let's look at what that means: Say you get a $500,000 loan and it funds. You make payments for three years, leaving a balance of $350,000. Now, even though you have paid off $150,000, you can't go back and get $150,000 in "new money." The only way to get that $150,000 is to take out a new first lien loan or a second lien loan with all the accompanying fees and costs.

SECRET

If you want to get revolving money on a real estate loan, take the proceeds and pledge them as collateral on a line of credit (LOC). Then you can pay and borrow, pay and borrow, etc. An additional huge benefit is that most LOCs are only for one year, but this one will always be renewed – so long as the collateral is healthy.

Tip No. 16 – Earn Interest on Your Collateral

When you use cash as collateral for a loan, have the bank pay you whatever it wants on the CD and charge you 1 point more for your loan. That way, the loan is costing you only 1 percent, because the bank is essentially paying you interest on the collateral.

In addition, when you use a CD as collateral on a loan, consider where you want the interest from that CD to be paid. Often it's added back into the CD, which will increase the interest you receive, but then it can't be used to go toward the interest you're paying the bank. **Consider having that interest paid into a money-market account, then using it to make the payment on the loan that the CD secures.** Ron has an arrangement like this and it leaves his net borrowing cost at 1 percent.

SECRET

Tip No. 17 – Watch for Prepayment Penalties and Hedges

Check your real estate loan documents carefully. Laws vary by state, but in many, the lender can charge you a **pre-payment penalty if you pay your loan off early.** This can be a pretty big fee, so think carefully before agreeing to it. As previously mentioned, Ron recently paid off a loan that he didn't realize had a pre-payment penalty in it. The cost was $125,000 on a $1.5 million loan – and he only paid it off to refinance it. (At the same bank!)

TRAP

SECRET

Also, **banks may hedge or match fund your loan.** That means they "match" your loan with a funding source, or hedge it in the markets that the rate won't go up or down too much to protect their exposure on rates. It's pretty complicated (too complex to explain fully here), but just ask if your loan is being hedged or match funded and what the implications might be to you. They may insist on a pre-payment penalty because they can't "unwind" the hedge or match funding with out a penalty. For instance, if you are paying 7 percent interest, and you pay off early, they may be in an environment where they can only loan the money at 3 percent, so they want to be made whole or not have the risk associated with the difference.

TRAP

Ron adds, "OMG!, I recently encountered **a car loan with a prepayment penalty** in the boilerplate. I was infuriated, but couldn't change it. Though I say toiling over the boilerplate is an exercise in futility, you should make sure there isn't anything there unexpected or unusual. I've NEVER seen a prepayment penalty on a car loan. You are likely to wreck or want to sell a car before the loan is paid off, so this can be important. The banks' attorneys are always coming up with things to add to the boilerplate based on isolated issues and lawsuits, so be it, and the banks of course are always looking for new sources of income. This one is bound to creep into more loans, that fee is immediate income, whereas many of the fees like origination fees must be amortized over the life of the loan for the lender."

Tip No. 19 – Choose the Legal Entity to Maximize Tax Benefits and Minimize Costs

SECRET

TRAP

Make sure you get legal and tax advice on this one, but one tactic I used was **to place real estate title in a single member LLC. I was doing a 1031 tax deferred transaction,** but I believe you can do this in most any case. It must be a single member LLC, however. You can then sell or convey the entity to another party without getting a new title policy, as the title policy belongs to the entity. **If you put it in your name personally, the coverage is lost when the property is conveyed.**

Tip No. 20 – Use the 10 Percent Rule

SECRET

Most lenders won't tell you unless you ask. But they have a 10 percent rule. This is fairly simple, most **banks can loan you 10 percent of what you already owe without a formal approval process.** Now don't misunderstand me, the loan still has to be underwritten and viable and all the fundamentals in place, but using this can save time, and in some cases money. You, of course, must be in good standing, and have a good relationship with the officer. An example? You have a $100,000 line of credit, and a $350,000 real estate loan, and $100,000 in truck loans, so total debt is $550,000. If your need is reasonable, you can usually get your line of credit raised by up to $55,000 without a formal request process. This is subject to your loan officer's authority of course and subject to the legal lending limit of the bank, among other things, but don't be afraid to ask.

❖ ❖ ❖ ❖ ❖

Chapter 9

A Few Words on Success

Final Thoughts from a Banker and an Entrepreneur

As important as the information in this book may be, it's only part of a much bigger picture. Success as a businessperson — regardless of field — depends on many components and learning how all the moving parts fit together can make the difference between success and failure. You won't find many tips, traps or secrets highlighted in this chapter, as this chapter is almost completely advice which includes all of those.

Although Ron and Greg have similar values, their backgrounds couldn't be more dissimilar. Greg has a BBA from Southern Methodist University and holds an MBA from Texas Christian University; Ron found himself living on his own as a teenager after his father's death and is largely self-educated. As different as these two men are, both have earned success in their fields through hard work, a laser-sharp focus on their goals and the desire to constantly improve their skills and knowledge.

Their approaches are as different as their backgrounds, but both have plenty to say about building a successful business.

Final Lesson – Get Rich Slowly

Greg: One thing that ties together everything we've talked about is an understanding that the prosperity of any nation depends upon the prosperity of its people. We can't do well as a country unless we learn to do well as individuals.

If America is a great nation, it's because of the prosperity of the people. Right now, we're not doing so well. Unemployment is up and a lot of people are facing hard times.

Debt can be your enemy, because it creates an illusion of wealth. You have debt so you get a loan and suddenly you don't feel like you're in debt any longer, because you have all this money available to you. I can tell you that banks hate to make debt consolidation loans, because after we put together a package and take care of those credit card bills, the next thing we see is that same customer is back needing a new loan, because now he or she has charged the cards all the way back up.

As a banker, when that happens, I realize that I should have practiced tough love the first time around and not made the loan. I should have made the customer learn instead. The point is that people who want to succeed and who want this country to succeed, have to learn to be good stewards of their money. They have to practice doing well with what they have before they think about someone lending them more.

Stewardship comes in a lot of ways. It means working harder than you're paid to work. Your task, not the clock, should determine your quitting time. A good employee and a good businessperson, doesn't work by the clock; he or she works to accomplish his or her goals.

Another place where I see people going wrong is that they don't pay themselves. Every person should put 10 percent of his or her pay in some sort of savings account. If you start doing that right out of college, it's easy to do for the rest of your life. But if you don't do that from the time you get your first job, it's going to be hard to turn into a habit. I'm telling you, though, that over time it'll add up to a significant amount of money.

Another way to practice better stewardship of your money is to take advantage of your company's 401(k) plan. If your company has a 401(k) plan and matches your contributions and you don't take advantage of that, you're crazy. That's free money! If someone is handing you money, you can't afford not to take it. Plus, it lowers your taxable income, so it benefits you all the way around. I have employees who'll say that they just can't afford to put that 6 percent of their income into the account; when I give them a raise, I try to get them to dedicate their raise to their 401k or other savings.

And as far as not being able to contribute to an IRA or 401k, it speaks directly to controlling expenses. First, you have to create a budget. If you can measure it, you can manage it. If you don't have a budget, you don't know where your money is going. We have people who come into the bank and make $400,000 a year, but don't have any idea where that money is going. There's no excuse for that.

Once you've made a budget, stick to it. If you can't afford to go out to eat, don't do it. It's just that simple. Saving money is similar to going on a diet. Everyone knows the key to a diet is eating fewer calories and exercising more. The key to savings is spending less and making more. Dieting and saving are easy to explain, but hard to put into practice.

Now that you're holding on to your money, learn to invest it wisely. Don't put it under your mattress and don't get into schemes. Seek competent financial advice and put your money where it can do the most good. You work all day, so you should let your money go to work, too. Diversify your investments and don't jeopardize your nest egg by putting it all in one basket.

Savings Pyramid

How an investor should deploy their savings.

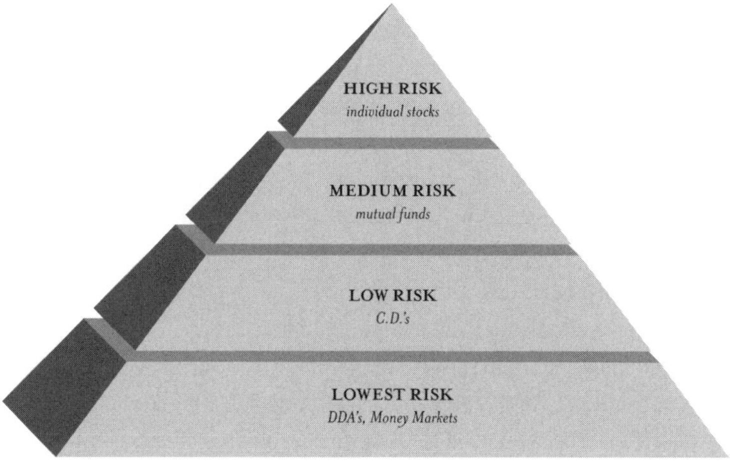

Remember that a small return is better than a complete loss. I would rather earn 1 percent on a CD than lose money in the market. Another wise thing to do is to invest in a house. I see people who are paying $1,800 in rent; it makes much more sense to get a mortgage so that they can build wealth and help their credit report.

Finally, always try to increase your ability to learn. If you increase your ability to learn, you'll increase your ability to earn. Go to trade meetings; get a personal coach; do whatever it takes to keep growing. If you're not growing as an individual, neither are your employees. And because your employees will follow the leader, you want to make sure you're taking them in the right direction.

Ron: I agree with what Greg says, because all of that is true. But at the same time, I understand that the people who are reading this are entrepreneurs. And as a whole, entrepreneurs have a lot more dreams than they have money. I understand that; I came from zero money and the only way I earned anything was by learning to leverage whatever I could get my hands on.

When you have no money, you have to learn how to use other people's money and that's what I did. I used money from lawyers, loan sharks and banks, the lender of last resort (IRS) and then leveraged every bit of it. But I was smart about how I did it; I didn't try to do it overnight and I let my business grow in small increments. In hindsight, not all of my ideas were good, such as borrowing from the IRS.

If we do only what is perfect, insure everything possible, pay every tax with no planning to minimize and do exactly what the government and other stakeholders expect of us, we will never get our business opened. Most entrepreneurs just don't have that kind of money going for them. So I think that is where Greg and I differ most in that I believe in using more leverage to get what you want. I believe in using credit, but I also believe in doing exactly what I say I'm going to do, when I say I'm going to do it.

You have to learn to move with a tremendous sense of urgency and focus, cautiously and judiciously and to do what I've done: Educate yourself on what you need to know to survive in business. I've learned enough about dealing with bankers to be able to write this book.

Like a lot of entrepreneurs, I understand what it's like to make payroll on my Visa card. I know what it's like not to be able to pay all the taxes. The IRS is the lender of absolute last resort and I have had to use it. I'm not proud of it, but it's what I had to do at the time.

Greg would say you should never, ever do that and he's right. But there are times when an entrepreneur can't do all the right things — when there aren't enough financial resources to do what "should" be done.

One of the ways to make up for those lean times is by working really smart and really hard. That's something that people really need to pay attention to right now. It tickles me that when things get bad, a lot of people say they need time off. They take off a week to go to Cancun. That's the wrong thing to do. When times are hard, that's when you'll find me at my desk around the clock, working. You shouldn't react to pressure by "getting away" — that's when you need to work harder. If you can't get a fire in your belly for success, you likely won't achieve that success. You can't put out a fire at your office if you're sitting on the beach.

My friends and competitors used to say that most folks shot the gun and then laid it down and that I just kept shooting. Frankly, it's hard to beat a competitor, even a marginal one that loves what they do and does it 12 hours a day for six days a week. I realize folks have to have a balance, but don't use it as an excuse to go home. I don't know anyone successful that works less than 50 or 60 hours a week and most work at least some Saturdays and all do some work from home. At least in the initial years.

If I had to summarize the tools I've used to become successful and not all are financial, they are: (not in any order)

1. Always do EXACTLY what you say you will, to EVERYONE. Tell it like it is. Under promise and over deliver. Always use a soft deadline; NEVER give out the hard deadline.

2. Surround yourself with people that are smarter than you. Yes,

they will work for you, because they have a high aversion to risk and could NEVER do what you are doing.

3. Surround yourself with people that can do what you don't, won't or shouldn't do, or that can do it better than you.

4. Become an effective leader. Not a boss, a leader. Attend a seminar a quarter, four per year, on something related to management and leadership.

5. Have a mantra of constant development and improvement. Read a book a month. Dog ear pages, make notes, make sure you have take-aways, executable ideas. Be passionate and have a sense of urgency about using what you learn. No matter how fast you move, it won't be fast enough. If you read eight best sellers on marketing you will be 80 percent as smart as the marketing guys that want to take all your money for helping you. The same applies for other genres of knowledge.

6. Be technologically savvy. You dont have to be on the bleeding edge, but don't be a pothole in the information highway. In 1992, I was carrying a pocket electronic Rolodex. I had contact information on everyone I came in contact with. It was a joke; everyone called me to get other people's numbers. Today, I use an iPhone and I know what "page rank" is on Google, use Facebook to network and have a Twitter identity. I am almost 60 years old, so that's unusual. Using technology will allow you to be more efficient, network, be more credible and visible and give you lots of bandwidth for projects and initiatives.

7. You simply must keep perfect credit. If you can't pay the balance on a credit card, pay the minimum amount due. Pay it ON TIME. My credit file has records dating back to 1979 and it's perfect. Bankers don't have time or patience for "stories," they want results. Be known as the client that is always moving fast and handling business and staying in front of the problems. The bankers love me because I am credible, entertaining, VERY candid, I call it like it is and they can count on my results. And oh, they make a lot of money on me. Don't try to beat every banker out of every quarter point. You

want them to point at you in the lobby and say "there's one of our best customers, we make a lot of money on him."

8. Understand the financials and operating metrics. Track them and study them relentlessly. I know its boring and sucks, but do it. Get someone that's smarter than you to help you understand it and present it to you, if you just can't get it, but YOU must present to the lenders and you must have an air of confidence and control when you present. You can't B.S. bankers. (Well, not too much – Sorry Greg)

9. Rely on peers and other professionals, including consultants, to help you, being judicious about the cost of course. I attribute a large part of my success to a peer-mentoring group I joined in 1988. The participants grew to have the largest and most successful operations in the U.S. and all sold out for big money when public companies came looking. You don't know what you don't know and you can learn it from others. I currently facilitate peer-mentoring groups and am expanding that practice to other industries; there are very few operators or industries that couldn't benefit from this service. That's a shameless pitch for my consulting practice (see the next tip).

10. Be willing to promote yourself, talk about your successes and mentor others, sharing. What goes around comes around. Some will resent your self-promotion, but they are the minority.

11. Learn marketing and advertising. Sure you need good products and services, but without good marketing you will likely fail or under achieve. Know your customers. Have a unique selling proposition. Make the customer king; be sincere and passionate about it. If you aren't creative, find someone to help you in this area

12. Learn to think strategically. I know this sounds simple, but it isn't. You have to be ahead of EVERYONE to get the results you want. You simply must build a discipline to stop and think before virtually every decision or action, how will this decision affect the next thing? And then what will happen? Then what will happen? ... then what will the result be? Is that the result I want? If not how can I influence it NOW instead of having to deal with it later?

13. There is no substitute for an extreme sense of urgency. Don't

wait to do it, do it now. Delegate it. Make it happen. You know already intuitively that no matter how fast you move in the world of business it's not fast enough. Practice the urgency every day. Every week. Every month. Be tireless; make sure everyone around you knows that you always wanted it yesterday. Their sense of urgency leverages on yours. Why wait months to get a new marketing design? Do it this week. Why wait to shake down the reason for high expenses in your service department? Do it today, get started, ask someone for all the metrics and reports for your review by this Thursday!

14. Be the 80 percent person. My peers used to love that I could get things done in a fraction of the time others needed. A SMALL fraction from my colleagues when I worked for 18 months at Ford Motor Co. I was decisive, relentless, passionate and results-oriented with a terrible sense of urgency. But my real secret was that most of the time you can get 80 percent of the results with 50 of the effort. We spend piles of time analyzing, noodling, baking, thinking, discussing, meeting, building models, you get the drift. Be quick on your feet, gather the relevant metrics and DO IT. You can always cycle back and make minor changes; you were never going to get 100 percent of the results quickly or painlessly anyway.

15. Host weekly meetings with all key employees. Have an agenda. Review it; require reports from each one on what they got done since last week's meeting and what they will get done next week. I keep my agenda in my iPhone and add to it each week as I walk around and or think of things. The morning of the meeting, I sync the phone and print it out; it takes less than 15 minutes weekly to do the agenda. You will be amazed how busy everyone gets the day before the meeting to make sure they can report out DONE the next day. Employees love structure, don't let them B.S. you otherwise.

16. Learn to delegate; tolerate mediocrity and the value of five seconds. First, you can't do it all. I know you can do it better then them, but it doesn't matter, they trust you to run the company, so

they get a check. Yes it will take them longer and it won't be as good or the same as if you had done it, but it is what it is, if you want to grow delegate. Don't delegate important matters because you want to go golfing, that sets a bad example. Yes, you will have to tolerate mediocrity. Learn to value time, if you can invest two hours today to save 10 minutes per week for the rest of your career, do it, even if it pains you. And never underestimate the value of saving 20 seconds, because when you do it over and over, it starts looking like an hour or more pretty quick, just think, would you like to have an extra hour per week?

17. Share with others, listen, be collaborative – you simply don't know what you don't know. I wish I had done more of this when I was younger.

18. Don't be afraid to be a rebel – Push back, think out of the box, but be strategic and analytic about it.

19. There's plenty of money. Be patient and prove you can plan and then execute against a plan. Be accountable. Wait for the Money Truck to back up!

20. Don't create a solution for a problem that doesn't exist and don't breathe your own exhaust (get enamored by your own ideas excluding others).

21. Watch and understand your competitors but don't focus on them. Use the energy to do what's right for your venture.

22. Positive energy – There is no other way to survive the grueling crawl to success.

23. Systems run like watches, people can let you down. It's important, especially as you grow, to install robust scalable systems that you can monitor and gather metrics on. People have a tendency to let you down, but systems prop everything up and allow you to know quickly when things are broken. For instance, I like requiring salespersons to write on a white board their results for the day, at the end of the day. How many calls did they take, how many outbound calls did they make, how many quotes did they give and how many

Backing the truck up – A reference to the figurative or literal vehicle that will be delivering proceeds (money) from a transaction. When the money truck hits us or arrives at our door, it means the transaction has closed and the money has arrived. Often the money *truck is backing up* but is not ready to unload, which can be frustrating. In most deals, the money truck backs up several times before it finally arrives (hitting us). Many businesspeople are superstitious about discussing it until the money is actually in hand. (See also: *money truck*.)

Use: "Bob felt that the *truck would back up* next Tuesday, and the closing would occur at 2 p.m. on that day; 'In this business, you never know for sure,' he said."

invoices did they write. Just some high level metrics that you can see when you walk past the board. If you have electronic systems, great, but make sure reports get distributed so everyone knows how things are going. You need systems for making the phone ring, for production or order fulfillment, leads generation, etc. Oftentimes systems will allow you to know sooner rather than later that things arent working. And sometimes you don't know what's right, but you know what's wrong, so if most new salespersons write 10 invoices on their first day and your new one today only writes two, you know that's wrong and more training may be needed.

24. Understand how your world is going to change – Many successful people start businesses, but their skills were limited to what they *did*. Chefs cook great and they may even be great leaders in the kitchen. But it's important to understand in a new role as owner that the employees are counting on you to *run the restaurant*. They know you can cook; it's not enough. Can you hire and fire, deal with clients, do the marketing, bring the clients, handle the legal stuff and keep track of the money. Until you've learned those skills, you are going to be frustrated and your team will be frustrated and you won't be an effective leader. Remember, they are counting on you to be *the* leader. It took you years to learn to cook, but you won't have years to learn all the rest of the stuff!

25. Do hard stuff first and have a good work ethic and a strong sense of urgency.

26. Have "positive dissatisfaction" about everything.

27. If you make me look good and I make you look good, then we will both always look good. Apply it and teach it, demand it.

TIP

People who do everything in the most conservative way will never open a business because they're afraid to take a risk. It's part of how we're made; as a banker, Greg's aversion to risk is much different than mine. Most bankers cannot stomach the risks that entrepreneurs take every day.

Part of what makes me a good entrepreneur is that my aversion to risk is lower than a banker's. I'm willing to take chances and I'm willing to borrow money to do it. Bankers are willing to loan me money because they like me as a customer.

You need both sides of the equation. Entrepreneurs need to understand where the banker is coming from, because the banker isn't always going to look at business the way we see it. But if the entrepreneur can understand what the banker needs and learn how to meet those needs, the relationship can work. The bottom line is, the banker and the businessperson need each other. Like any relationship, it's about figuring out how to give each one what he or she needs for that relationship to be able to grow.

Index

D

E

F

G

H

I

J

K

L

M

S

T

U

V

W

About the Author

Ron Sturgeon

As founder of Mr. Mission Possible small business consulting, Ron Sturgeon combines more than 35 years of entrepreneurship with an extensive background in consulting, speaking, and publishing.

A business owner since age 17, Ron sold his chain of salvage yards to Ford Motor Company in 1999, and his innovations in database-driven direct marketing have been profiled in Inc. Magazine. After the repurchase of Greenleaf Auto Recyclers from Ford and sale to Schnitzer Industries, Ron is now owner of the DFW Elite Auto suite of businesses and a successful real estate investor. This is Ron's 4th business book.

As a consultant and peer benchmarking leader, Ron shares his expertise in strategic planning, capitalization, compensation, growing market share, and more in his signature plain-spoken style, providing field-proven, high-profit best practices well ahead of the business news curve. To learn more about Ron, visit his main site, www.MrMissionPossible.com.

About the Author

Greg Morse

Greg Morse was raised in West Texas where he had several small businesses and jobs as a teenager. He went on to Southern Methodist University where he pretty much paid his own way. After receiving an undergraduate degree in finance, he became a commercial lender at a large financial institution and continued, at night, to obtain his MBA from Texas Christian University. Upon receiving his graduate degree, he continued his banking career, but also taught upper-level and graduate-level finance courses at the University of Texas in Arlington. His classes were asked to vote on a charity to which he would donate his teaching compensation. Greg also has a graduate degree from the Southwestern Graduate School of Banking at Southern Methodist University and is presently CEO of the bank he founded as one of the few remaining locally-owned, independent banks. Learn more about Greg at the bank's site, www.WorthingtonBank.com

❖ ❖ ❖ ❖ ❖

The authors met each other about five years before they knew each other. Sound strange? Well, Ron had a reputation for being an entrepreneur with a keen sense of banking and Greg had an excellent reputation for being a banker with an entrepreneurial spirit. Since Ron's business was always handled by another loan officer at the banks where Greg worked, the two weren't given the chance to work together. But once Greg instituted a bank, he decided that he and Ron really needed to meet, in person.

Good Books Make Great Gifts…

Straight-forward, informative, and very useful, Greg Morse and Ron Sturgeon's new book Getting to Yes with Your Banker makes a thoughtful gift for a business associate, friend or family member.

- **Of permanent value** – Ron Sturgeon and Greg Morse's new book is a roadmap for getting the most from your business banking relationships.

- **Personalized** – Autographed and gift-inscribed copies available. Customize the cover or jacket with the name of your firm.

- **Practical and Actionable** – Greg Morse and Ron Sturgeon have the experience to give you the inside skinny on the world of small business lending. Practical, easy-to-follow advice for getting to yes.

Quantity discounts available.

Order gift copies today
by visiting

www.GettingToYesWithYourBanker.com

Order Form

Online Orders:	www.GettingToYesWithYourBanker.com
E-Mail Orders:	orders@GettingToYesWithYourBanker.com
Postal Orders:	visit website Contact Us page for address
Fax Orders:	(817) 838-8477
Phone Orders:	(817) 999-0980
By Mail:	5940 Eden, Ft. Worth TX 76117

Title	Price	Quantity	Subtotal
Getting to Yes with Your Banker	$19.95	______	______
	Sales Tax*		______
	Shipping & Handling**		______
	TOTAL		______

*Sales Tax: Please add 8.25% tax for products shipped to TX addresses.

**Shipping and Handling: (US) Add $4 for first product and $2 for each additional product. Call for international pricing.

Shipping:

Name: ______________________________

Address: ______________________________

City, State Zip: ______________________________

Telephone: ______________________________

E-Mail Address: ______________________________

Payment:

❑Check enclosed ❑ VISA ❑ MasterCard

Card Number: ______________________________

Exp. Date: ______________________________

Security Code: ______________________________

Signature: ______________________________

Name on card: ______________________________

Billing Address: ______________________________

City, State Zip: ______________________________

Personalized Gift for Your Clients

A Great Premium Gift

Makes a great gift for lending institutions, for clients or prospects. What a great way to show prospects and customers you care!

We can put a label on the cover of the book personalized to your specifications, stating that the book is a gift from your firm, or as you see fit for the label. We can also modify cover to your specifications, on larger quantities, please inquire.

We can also offer fulfillment from your list, please inquire about these services.

Quantity pricing is as follows.

(All are plus freight, advance payment)

Call 817-999-0980 for a personalized quote.

Book pricing as premium gift:

Discount
10% 3-10 copies
20% 11-25 copies
25% 26-50 copies
30% 51-200 copies
40% 201-500 copies
Inquire 501 or more copies

Prices and discounts subject to change without notice.